| | **DATE DUE** | | 5/01 |
|---|---|---|---|
| JUN 23 '01 | | | |
| JUL 18 '01 | | | |
| AUG 10 '01 | | | |
| AUG 31 '01 | | | |
| SEP 25 '01 | | | |
| OCT 04 '01 | | | |
| SEP 20 '02 | | | |
| | | | |
| | | | |
| | | | |
| | | | |
| | | | |
| | | | |
| | | | |
| | | | |
| | | | |
| | | | |
| GAYLORD | | | PRINTED IN U.S.A. |

*The Final Season*

# The
# *Final*
# *Season*

FATHERS,

SONS, AND

ONE LAST

SEASON IN

A CLASSIC

AMERICAN

BALLPARK

*Tom Stanton*

THOMAS DUNNE BOOKS
ST. MARTIN'S PRESS
NEW YORK

THOMAS DUNNE BOOKS.
An imprint of St. Martin's Press.

www.stmartins.com

All photos courtesy of the author's personal collection, unless otherwise noted.

Design by Susan Walsh

ISBN 0-312-27288-X

First Edition: June 2001

Printed in the United States of America

10  9  8  7  6  5  4  3  2  1

*For Joe and Betty Stanton*

*The Final Season*

Navin Field, 1920s. Photo courtesy of Burton Historical Collection, Detroit Public Library.

# Preface

**October 2000** ◇ Theodore Stankiewicz died in 1957, three years before I was born. Everything I know about him—from his beloved rosebushes to his thorny temper—I have learned from others. As a boy I visited the home on Montlieu Street where he and Grandma had spent most of their lives and cared for their ten children. On scattered Sundays we'd stop for pierogi and kielbasa and to reminisce with Uncle Teddy, who inherited the house and lived in it through the 1970s, eventually putting bars on the windows.

I never felt more connected to Grandpa than at his house.

In the cool basement, I could imagine him bottling Prohibition beer and cutting cabbage for the sauerkraut crock. In the kitchen I could picture him playing late-night pinochle, rapping his knuckles on the table in victory, the air heavy with smoke. I could see him in the yard cutting flowers to take to Mount Olivet Cemetery, where he had buried two young daughters, and I could hear him in the attic screaming at his son Clem for marking the walls with the names of Earl Whitehill and Ownie Carroll, Tiger pitchers.

Old buildings bring life to stories. They put a foundation to memories. They link you to the past and help you feel rooted.

In January 1999 on a bright Saturday morning after picking out seats at Tiger Stadium, Dad and I left the security of the freeway and ventured past boarded storefronts down to Montlieu near Detroit's small city airport. I drove slowly and

Dad, then seventy-nine, looked side to side, squinting at the occasional house, at brick porches and elm trees, searching for something familiar, a landmark from his youth, something that would tell him where he was and where he had been. Finally he motioned at a vacant lot, flanked by other vacant lots and across from a crumbling house. The home had stood there. But without the walls, without the French doors, without roses in the yard, without something to touch, the bond had frayed to threads.

I kept driving.

The Stankiewicz men—Grandpa, his sons, and their boys—have long loved baseball, and living in Detroit they have felt a special affection for the Tigers. For 105 years the city's professional team played on the grounds of a former hay market at Michigan and Trumbull Avenues, first at Bennett Park, then Navin Field, Briggs Stadium, and Tiger Stadium.

Wherever there are ballparks, there are memories.

Mine feature colorful uncles who a decade ago began their procession into old age. Bohemians and roughnecks, plant workers and radical activists—in hindsight Grandma must have seen the humor in naming them for saints. By the start of the 1999 season, two of her sons, Teddy and Clem, had passed on. Another, Bucky (none of us calls him Edward), could no longer travel from his home in California. We were unsure about Herb and Tommy. If alive, Herb probably lived in South Korea, we guessed. As for Tommy, the youngest one, the kind, quiet fellow for whom I was named, he had withdrawn from our lives twenty-seven years earlier, leaving a void that my father, Joe, struggled to fill.

I could never go to Tiger Stadium without feeling the ghosts of history about me, without imagining my grandpa walking the same dank, dark concourse that ran beneath the stands. I couldn't help but picture Uncle Bucky as one of a legion of lucky boys picking stones from the infield for Mr. Navin. Or

Uncle Teddy, a trusting soul who at sixteen defended Santa Claus in an alley fight, brushing cracked peanut shells from the scoresheets on which he precisely recorded games. Or Dad in his Air Corps uniform taking Tommy on a furlough adventure. And my own sons, the oldest edging toward manhood, calling to a ballplayer on the field and hoping for an autograph.

I felt the connection and I was not alone.

About a year ago, Tiger Stadium hosted its last game. The ballpark was retired and the team moved to a pristine facility, where the girders don't bleed rust. Someday—maybe in two years, maybe in ten—the old diamond will be erased from the landscape like our family home on Montlieu. The thought of losing that ballpark compelled me in April 1999 to embark on a mission that I had dreamt of as a child: attending all eighty-one home games. My friends grinned and shook their heads. Some were envious. Others thought I was crazy. I had done nothing so frivolous in my thirty-eight years, and I struggled to explain. Beth, my wife, sounded supportive. Did she realize that holidays, birthdays, and anniversaries would be spent at the park and that the team's schedule would dictate ours and that I'd be gone late into the night, day after day, for much of six months? Did she think this was my midlife crisis?

My sons liked the idea. What kids wouldn't recognize the joy in spending an eternity at the ballpark? In their eyes it was like traveling with the circus or working in an ice-cream parlor. The potential problems faded next to the glorious benefits. And with my dad, well, when it comes to baseball he's always been a kid and he's always supported me, even when he shouldn't have.

I didn't know what to expect from the experience. It was motivated by something I couldn't quite corner. Why would a man my age with family, a respectable job, and a stable psychological history obsess over an aging ballpark? That was the mystery, I guess, and I hoped to figure it out. You can be the judge of that. I approach these matters as I approach a brown bat trapped in the living room. Open a window and in time it finds its way out. This being a journal of an actual summer in the stands, I couldn't predict what the adventure would bring. This much I did know and still know today: There are places on earth that mean more than words and pictures can explain. Writer Willie Morris called them "terrains of the heart." They are the points on our personal maps where we find our treasured memories and replenish our hungering souls. For me, that was Tiger Stadium. If you're lucky, you have such a place, too, and perhaps you will understand.

◇ ◇ ◇ ◇ ◇ ◇  *April 1999*

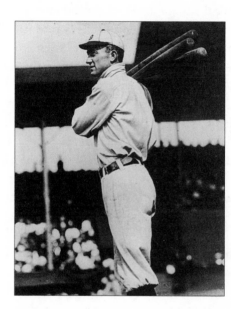

Ty Cobb. Photo courtesy of Burton Historical Collection, Detroit Public Library.

**Game 1: Monday, April 12** ◇ Eighty-seven years earlier on a Saturday in April 1912, days after the *Titanic* sank, the Detroit ball club played its first game on this diamond. It was called Navin Field and it was about half the size then, jammed with more than 24,300 fans. Cleveland's "Shoeless Joe" Jackson scored the inaugural run and Ty Cobb responded a half inning later by stealing home. The Tigers won 6–5 in eleven innings, christening a field that over the decades has hosted all the greats. Ruth and Gehrig. DiMaggio and Williams. Mantle, Mays, and Aaron. Nolan Ryan and Roger Clemens. Boston's Fenway Park opened the same day. They are America's oldest ballparks.

It was that year on a Tuesday in July when Theodore Stankiewicz, a twenty-six-year-old welder, married Anna Tuchewicz at St. Hyacinth Church in Detroit, beginning a union that would produce ten children and a thousand stories. Teddy, as pals called him, had fled Poland after being drafted into the German army. He followed his two brothers, who at six foot five stood nearly a foot taller. We know little about his life in Europe, except that he grew up on a farm and lost his father early. Anna, Teddy's bride, was eighteen. She worked in a cigar factory and like her younger siblings lived with her parents, a stern Catholic couple from Europe. Nine months after the wedding, they began their family. First Clem was born, then Edward, Theodore, and Irene. While expecting her fifth baby in early 1920, Anna took ill and lost her eyesight. She spent months in bed, watched over by her sisters and mother, saying rosaries and praying to Saint Anne to save her child, telling God that while she might not be worthy of His mercy, the baby should be spared. For Anna, every joy and every tragedy found its roots in her faith. In March when the child was born, her sight returned. She pronounced both as miracles and bestowed upon her son, my father, the most sacred name she could imagine, Joseph Marion.

Generations of Detroiters have watched baseball at Michigan and Trumbull Avenues. My grandfather cheered Cobb and "Wahoo" Sam Crawford. As a teen in the 1930s my dad packed peanuts beneath the bleachers for a chance to behold the G-Men: Gehringer, Greenberg, and Goslin. Later he took me to see Kaline. Now I take my sons and they have their own favorites. The tradition is not unique to us.

Game time is a good hour away when Bobby Higginson strides to the bench after batting practice, his unsmiling lips framed by a tight goatee.

"Hand this to him," he says, pointing the barrel of his black baseball bat at an unsuspecting boy two rows back. Higginson, an intense right fielder prone to outbursts, slides the cracked bat over the glossy roof of the Tiger dugout. He pauses, watching that it gets to Mickey Bozymowski, and disappears down the steps into the clubhouse.

The boy holds the bat like a sacred sword. He caresses its neck, sticky with pine tar, and looks up to his dad, who says, "Oh man!" Michael Bozymowski has been a baseball fan since the 1960s. "Oh man!" he says. "I don't believe this."

The team's most popular player has anointed Michael Bozymowski's son, at the home opener no less. Does Higginson realize that he has etched a moment into one family's history—that in sixty years Mickey Bozymowski will be recalling this day for his grandchildren? Mickey's dad knows it. He grins, shakes his head, and lets his eyes drift over the grass field.

"I just had to be here," he says.

Nearby, Alan Trammell, the former shortstop and first-year batting coach, gives autographs at the edge of the dugout and a knot of fans tightens toward him. In 1978 as I was finishing high school, Trammell was beginning his first full season. He and Lou Whitaker were the Golddust Twins. On this Monday in spring, with his shades perched on the bill of his ball cap, he looks younger than forty-one. He is trim, and boyish in the face. The acne scars of his youth have smoothed.

"You the man, Al," someone shouts.

Trammell signs a baseball and politely excuses himself. "I've got to go to work now," he says, as if he needs to explain.

The park is a circus of sound. The click of ball meeting bat echoes from the batting cage. The Jumbotron screen over center field blares highlights of last year's Sammy Sosa–Mark McGwire home-run race.

"Ice-cold beer," yells an unpracticed vendor, the words

strange on his tongue. "Wash down the pretzels. Wash down that popcorn. Ice-cold beer."

Few are buying yet. The veteran, Art Witkosky, knows this. He resembles a white-haired Johnny Cash and the only thing he is selling at this moment is himself. Witkosky hoists a bag of buns above his head, posing for the press. Though he's been hawking hot dogs since Nixon's presidency, Witkosky never tires of opening day.

Above home plate in the WJR radio booth, Hall of Famer Ernie Harwell prepares for his broadcast. Harwell is one of my boyhood idols, a fatherly figure I listened to in bed in the dark on late summer evenings, with the Tigers playing on the West Coast and the signal coming in clear on the transistor radio and the crickets chirping outside my window. I imagine him a considerate man and I hope to meet him. Callously fired years earlier, Harwell, eighty-one, has returned to do play-by-play, his fortieth Detroit season. In a Greek sailor's cap and tan overcoat, he settles into the open-air booth behind fencing that protects him from foul balls, lest he meet the fate of H. G. Salsinger, the late sportswriter who took a blinding ball to the face in 1954 and never returned to the park.

Today Harwell's unhurried voice, hinting at his Georgia childhood, floats from the radio, slow and sweet and sincere as a mother's praise.

"Baseball greetings, everybody, from The Corner. It'll be the last time we say that on an opening day. This is a great occasion and the weatherman has blessed us with some good weather. It is sunny. It's not warm; it's cool. But it's sunny and we are very thankful for that."

Wind snaps the American League team pennants that line the roof of the stadium like flags atop a castle. Tiger Stadium is a double-deck fortress, the only major-league park encircled by two levels of stands. From almost all seats you can see nothing outside the park, no landmarks, no buildings, no cars.

Just the sky, the seagulls, and several planes circling above trailing banners that read, *Think Ford First, Ron's Body Shop and Suspension,* and *Deja Vu's Totally Nude Showgirls.* The park embraces you.

In the upper deck along the right-field foul line, it is cold in the shade, colder than the announced game-time temperature of 47 degrees. Fans with ski hats and winter gloves struggle to get warm. A woman trudges up the narrow chipped steps in a fuzzy feline costume and my dad gives her a second look.

He sits to my right so I can talk into his hearing aid. He's got eyeglasses as big as flight goggles. Somehow you can see the kid in him.

"Never been up here before," he says.

Dad has been coming to games since the 1920s when his father bought tickets with the extra change he earned brewing coffee during lunch breaks at the Chrysler plant. In Poland Theodore Stankiewicz had never heard of baseball. In America he worshiped it, spending more time at ball fields than in the eastside Catholic churches where his children were baptized. When he arrived in America, the Tigers played at Bennett Park, named for Charlie Bennett, a star catcher who lost his legs in a streetcar accident. Bennett Park came down in 1911, replaced by the larger Navin Field, to accommodate the burgeoning city of immigrants and the demand to see Ty Cobb, the American League's top hitter and fiercest competitor. The park expanded several times, doubling in size by 1938 and taking the name of new owner Walter Briggs.

It was Briggs Stadium when Harold "Prince Hal" Newhouser made it to the big leagues after his senior year in high school. Newhouser lived in the city and starred on local teams. Before he became a pro he had pitched for Roose-Vanker, the American Legion state champions. My dad batted against him in a single game that has become part of family legend.

Two years ago Dad, my brother, and I came for the retirement of Newhouser's uniform number, 16. On the drive down Dad said he felt like a boy. Then he paused, stared off through the tinted car window and exhaled with a subtle, satisfying "hmmm."

"Sometimes when I'm shaving, I don't recognize myself in the mirror," he said. "I see an old man."

For the ceremony Dad stood by the dugout, camera in hand. When Newhouser, in poor health, stepped onto the field, Dad edged closer to the diamond. I think he hoped that his former adversary would spot him in the crowd of thousands and recognize him as the wily second baseman who sixty years earlier had spoiled his sandlot no-hitter with two bloop hits that rolled into the crowd for ground-rule doubles. Weeks earlier, before the ceremony, Dad had sent him a letter recalling their encounter. Who could expect Newhouser to remember? He had gone on to face some of baseball's best hitters. He had gone on to pitch in All-Star games and the World Series. He had even been the American League's Most Valuable Player—twice.

But before that, when he was a fast-throwing phenom, he had had to face my dad and my dad had gotten the better of him. Grandpa Stankiewicz watched that scrub game with a cigar in his hand and two in his shirt pocket. He took pride in his son's hits.

"You swung on a line, Joe," he said.

Newhouser died last November. (He never did answer Dad's letter.) His number hangs on the facing of the third deck and whenever I look at it I think of my father.

In the bleachers awash in sunshine, shirtless young men punch beach balls into the breeze. Occasionally one drifts onto the field, halting the scoreless game between Willie Blair and Minnesota's Eric Milton. Some shutouts arise from precise control, an overpowering fastball, or a nice mix of pitches;

others result from lousy hitting. That's the case today and there is no worse scenario for an opener. The stands are packed with partygoers who hunger for celebration, not baseball. They'd be as happy at a demolition derby if there was beer. And I resent them for it because this should be a solemn, respectful time, not an excuse to get drunk.

A well-endowed woman flutters the bottom of her blouse, baiting the men who sit nearby. The fans to her right cheer. She looks to her left and swirls her arms into the air. The hoots and applause grow again. Inspired, she frolics into the aisle and fulfills her promise, hoisting her top over her jiggling head. Her admirers boo as police escort her from the park. One tosses a roll of toilet paper over the guardrail. It unfurls, a white, three-ply ribbon.

In the late innings several college-age men leap the outfield fences and dart onto the field, easily evading the middle-aged security guards who take care not to flop before a sellout crowd of over 47,000. One intruder trips near the Budweiser sign in left-center. Another slides bare-chested and headfirst into second base.

Everyone wants to be a star.

If this were a movie, Bobby Higginson would be at the plate with another black bat and Mickey Bozymowski would be big-eyed and hopeful. Instead it's Damion Easley, the second baseman, who finds himself where every ballplaying kid dreams of glory: bottom of the ninth, two out, the winning run on third, and the count at three balls, two strikes. Easley is poised to be the hero. The fans can feel it. They rise from their seats, their cheers building to thunder. But the not-so-mighty Easley strikes out.

Relief pitcher Todd Jones, with his bleached-blond goatee, enters in the tenth inning. He has on Al Kaline's Wilson A-2000 glove, the same glove Kaline used in 1974, his final season. "I just think something of his needs to be on that field," Jones said earlier. He pitches flawlessly. His successor, though, surrenders a twelfth-inning home run and the Tigers lose their sixth straight following a dismal start on the road.

"Tough loss," says Dad, as if I were a kid again who needed consoling.

On some level, I do. But not about the game.

—— **Minnesota 1** ◇ **Detroit 0** ——

*The Canyon*

Derek Jeter and Paul O'Neill.

**Game 2: Wednesday, April 12** ◊ This is the park as I've never seen it, hours before the contest, the stands vacant, the gates closed to paying fans. My press pass, issued reluctantly, gets me in early. The ball club is wary of my motives, with reason. I am angry that the team is abandoning the park and I don't feel fond of the people who made the decision. Still, I am tickled to be here today, even comforted in some way, and privileged, of course.

Emerging from the cement tunnel you notice the grass first, shamrock green. Perhaps it's the vastness of it, this huge flag of a field spread before you and hugged by a sea of blue seats, or the way the diagonal cut creates a pattern of alternating stripes, one bright, one dull, depending on the direction of the mower and where you're sitting. Or maybe it's just wishfulness; for green represents youth, vitality, and promise and they abound at a ballpark, in our spirits and minds if nowhere else.

Noises carry in an empty stadium. Across the field you can hear the pop of a ball in a glove. You can hear solitary voices, one sweeper griping to another, "I don't work for nothing." You can hear the sound system buzzing and the manager, Larry Parrish, chatting with a news reporter. You can hear Bryce Florie's disappointment as he tests his stiff shoulder in the bullpen and you can hear the silence of Californian Dave Weaver watching Florie with curiosity and compassion. Florie's injury is an opportunity for Weaver's son, called up from the Double A farm team. Jeff Weaver will start tonight's game, his first in the majors. The Tigers have big plans for Weaver, their top draft pick.

At game time the rookie, a six-foot-five blond kid, opens his major-league career with a hard fastball. Torii Hunter swings late and misses. When Hunter strikes out, the fans fill with hope.

"Weeea-ver! Weeea-ver!" yells one woman.

The team has been desperate for pitching—for nine years.

"A pitcher who throws strikes?" says a grandfather with an earring in his left lobe.

Out in the concourse, innings later, vendor Amzie Griffin removes a toothpick from the corner of his smile and says it's been a slow night, a typical early-in-the-season slow night. Griffin lays his hands on his glass display case.

"Look at these," he says spreading his fingers.

He tilts them to catch the light. His nails shine. They're immaculate, clipped and cleaned—maybe polished—not what you'd expect after a shift at Ford. Since 1960 Griffin has worked days at the auto company, and nights and weekends at the park. When he started, only whites sold hot dogs. Griffin and others protested. A year later they got a share of the lucrative dog market.

"But our nails had to be perfect," he says.

With his seniority Griffin has the pick of stadium vending jobs. He likes souvenir booth number 15 near the busy left-field gate, sandwiched between food counters and anchored across from the restrooms. His children once helped with the business. They're grown now. Tonight a friend's son assists him. The youth turns to Griffin and mumbles a question.

"Speak clearly so we can understand you," Griffin says. The teen needs change. Griffin pulls a wad of bills from his pocket and files through them for a five.

His booth sells everything from shot glasses to newborn gift sets with creeper caps, booties, and baseball-shaped teething rings.

"You don't make enough here to support a family," he says. "This is my hobby. When we close up in October, I start to count the days until April."

Sportservice, the company that employs Griffin and hundreds of others, will lose its contract after this year. The ball club will handle its own concessions in 2000. It'll be one more source of revenue for the team and possibly one less for guys like Amzie Griffin.

"Are they going to hire you?" I ask, giving the word "they" an indignant twist.

Griffin peeks over his reading glasses and looks at me as if I'm naive. He raises his eyebrows and taps his shiny nails on the counter.

"We'll see," he says.

—— **Detroit 7** ◇ **Minnesota 1** ——

Jeff Weaver coasts through five shutout innings, allowing one hit. Tomorrow the papers will proclaim him a "Dream Weaver."

**Game 3: Thursday, April 15** ◇ Howard Stone, sixty-two, waves us into his gravel lot, HK Service Parking, along Cochrane Avenue, a blacktopped road less inspiring than the ballplayer for which it was named. We pull in beside a minivan, leaving a comfortable three feet between vehicles.

"A little closer," Stone says, raising his hands so they're eighteen inches apart.

I nick the other guy's door getting out.

In 1953 Howard's dad, bar owner Harry Stone, bought several residential parcels, cleared them of their houses, and went into business, charging fifty cents a car. For forty-seven years, through high school, college, a career in education, and now retirement, Howard has been flagging vehicles. He guesses that he has spent four thousand days on this land, renting spaces for games he rarely sees.

Dozens of parking lots dot the landscape around the stadium, wedging thirty or forty cars onto front lawns and into narrow tracts between bars and storefronts. In the 1910s, in days before every household had an automobile, ballparks were built in neighborhoods, often on streetcar routes. Consequently no one had planned for parking at Tiger Stadium. It fell to small-time entrepreneurs to meet the need. I park in Stone's lot every game, a privilege that costs $648 for the season and puts me just outside gate 9, with quick access to the freeway. It's an ideal spot and it impresses my son Zack, thirteen.

Stone chatters like a salesman, cracking jokes that fall a few shades shy of off-color.

"Did you hear that the Lions signed a quarterback from Kosovo?" he begins.

Though a fan, he catches the Tigers only on the road. He spends home games with what must be the industry's most overqualified crew of parking attendants. A dentist. A podiatrist. An attorney. Teachers and coaches. They are his friends and family and they direct cars that have brought Nelson Mandela, Jake LaMotta, and Sandy Koufax.

In autumn when the stadium closes, Stone will be left with barren plots and there is no shortage of those in the Empowerment Zone near Rosa Parks Boulevard.

"It's not only a financial loss, it's my life," he says.

Zack, my oldest son, grows restless. At nearly six feet and two hundred pounds, he no longer disappears into my shadow. Stone sees him fidgeting.

"Hey, we'll talk more later," he says. "We've got the whole season."

Indeed we do, and I plan to share much of it with my three boys. I want them to remember the park that has meant so much to our family. Years from now I want them to point at the corner of Michigan and Trumbull and recall for their grandsons how their ancestors—all the way back to my grandfather, Polish immigrant Theodore Stankiewicz—shared the national pastime here through nine decades. I want them to know about Hal Newhouser and Charlie Gehringer and Al Kaline. I want them to remember.

In our family, baseball has always been a communion of dads, boys, and brothers. Mom never went to the park, not even before the brain surgeries that altered her life during my childhood. Neither did my grandmother. On any given day probably eight of ten fans at Tiger Stadium are male. Maybe it's because when our daughters exit the T-ball leagues of early childhood they are ushered into the segregated world of girls' softball. Maybe it's because no woman has played in the majors. Whatever the reason, baseball is mostly, though not entirely, a sport of fathers and sons.

To that, Brian Moehler can attest.

He pitches tonight. After his final warm-up, with the game about to begin, Moehler turns from home plate toward center field. He stands solemnly, his Detroit cap off, and bows his head for several seconds. Then he scrawls the letters *FM* into the reddish clay of the pitching mound. It's a ritual he carries out faithfully. Fred Moehler died in 1995, before his son Brian made the big leagues. Even at age twenty-seven Brian Moehler wants his father near him.

"Dad," says my son Zack, "did you know that one time a fly ball bounced off Jose Canseco's head?"

"Really?"

"Yeah. It went over the fence for a home run."

We've settled into our usual seats between home and third base. Section 217. Elmore Leonard's section. The author's not here on this cold overcast evening. Not many are. Fewer than 12,000 bought tickets and most skipped.

"Want another piece?" I ask Zack, opening the Little Caesars pizza box that warms my lap. Zack takes the bigger slice and scratches leftover cheese from the cardboard tray.

"Dad, did you know that Allan Sherman was the only comedian to have three number-one albums?"

We pass the game with questions. Zack loves trivia.

"Who was Michael Dukakis's running mate?"

In the fourth inning we move twenty rows behind home, where an out-of-shape security guard watches the players' wives. We have our pick of empty rows. I sit first. Zack sits two seats away. He leaves a spot vacant between us, which he has never done before.

"The seats are tighter here," he explains.

It reminds me of an eight-mile bike trip we took on Mackinac Island, a Lake Huron resort. Shortly into the ride Zack pulled out front and pedalled faster, leaving my wife, me, and his two younger brothers behind. He got so far ahead that he disappeared around a stony bend a quarter mile up the road. I could no longer see him and he apparently could not hear me. I realized then that it was a preview of our coming years, with him putting distance between us, and me struggling to stay close.

When he was four I would lay next to Zack on his bed and sing James Taylor's "Sweet Baby James" in the night's darkness, changing the words to "Sweet Zachary James" so convincingly that he may still think the song is about him. Recognizing the final notes he'd say, "One more time." I would sing until he fell asleep, his soft cheek near my heart.

I imagined we would always feel as close.

In fifth and sixth grades, he invited me to chaperon field trips. We went to Camp Talahi, to Chicago, to museums and parks. This year, when his eighth-grade science class headed to a cave in Indiana, Zack said no parents were going. When plans surfaced for a National Junior Honor Society trip to Toronto, he said all available seats were taken. In July he will spend a week at a university band camp. Another parent told me the school needs volunteers. Zack hasn't mentioned a word.

I know better than to be surprised by this. At thirteen I didn't want my dad on a field trip or at my school. I was born when he was forty. He had ten to fifteen years on my friends' fathers, a fact that bothered me. I did allow him to be part of my baseball life—or did he insist on it? We played catch in our suburban backyard, parallel to the rosebushes along the fence. He threw underhand—"submarine style," he called it—like

Elden Auker, a player from his youth. I threw hard and wild, the ball bouncing off his shins or scooting into the flowers behind him.

"Just throw it. Don't aim it," he would say.

He came to my St. Malachy games, watched me play short-stop, cheered my only home run, and contradicted his father by advising me never to swing at the first pitch.

"Charlie Gehringer didn't swing at the first pitch." To him Gehringer was the epitome of a great player. Quiet and disciplined. The Mechanical Man. His dedication to the sport, Dad said, had kept him a bachelor until he retired.

At the annual St. Malachy banquet fathers and sons celebrated the season's end. Some boys got trophies. Dad always came and one time he shared a few laughs with our manager, Ray Szydlak, whose right index finger and thumb were burnished a dirty yellow from pinching unfiltered cigarettes. Through the conversation, Dad jangled the coins in his pocket. I noticed immediately and I was certain everybody else did. He sifted those coins like a pirate sifts treasure. Every rattle and clatter, every clash of nickel against dime, quarter against penny, clanged like church bells. It didn't take much to embarrass me and here was my dad blowing whistles, crashing cymbals, and rolling on the floor. Or so it seemed.

I said something harsh.

Funny how memory serves its master, for I remember the coins but not my words. They must have been hurtful, though, for years later, when I was done with college, Dad caught himself clinking his change in my unforgiving presence. He grinned. "You don't like that, do you?"

Zack pulls me into the moment, oblivious to the insecurities swirling through me.

"Dad," he says. "There are fifty-two people in the bleachers."

I want to tell him that he should sit next to me, that I'm not ready for the distance, that it feels like a canyon and that it saddens me and that I'm already losing the ballpark. Yet no matter how I arrange the words, they sound weak.

"Fifty-two people," I say as if nothing is wrong. "That's pocket change for a ball club."

—— **Minnesota 8** ◇ **Detroit 6** ——

The Twins hammer Brain Moehler. Damion Easley scores twice and knocks in two on a single, a double, and a home run.

**Game 4: Friday, April 16** ◇ When the world champions swagger onto the field, kids in Yankee jerseys swarm the dugout for autographs. Middle-aged men call out to manager Joe Torre. Boys and young women crane their necks toward Derek Jeter, the shortstop from Kalamazoo. The Yankees are America's premier baseball team, winners of a record 114 games last season. They stand taller than their peers. They step with confidence. They throw harder, hit better, smile nicer. They almost glow.

I love the Yankees and I hate them. I love them because they have a glorious history, peopled with Ruths and Gehrigs and DiMaggios, and because they wear pinstripes, play so well, and win so often. Home team to the nation's biggest market, they have prospered since buying Babe Ruth in 1920. They have captured twenty-four of seventy-nine world championships and competed in another ten. No one comes close.

But the Yankees also represent the moneyed world of baseball that has splintered the sport into haves and have-nots and doomed parks like Tiger Stadium. The first six hitters in their lineup—Chuck Knoblauch, Jeter, Paul O'Neill, Bernie Williams, Tino Martinez, and Chili Davis—are paid $35.7 million. Detroit's entire twenty-five-player roster gets less. Williams alone makes almost $10 million a year, more than McGwire, Sosa, or Griffey, and no club exceeds the Yankees' $85-million payroll.

Most teams cannot compete with those salaries and that fact gives birth to the argument for new venues with luxury suites, parking structures, and biscotti bakeries. Our club got serious about forsaking this park in the early 1990s when the former team president scolded all who objected. "It's unfair for you to think that you can shackle us to a rusted girder...and expect us to compete and win," he said.

For a long while I struggled with how to argue the finances. That proved futile; a modern stadium will bring in more money and will allow the team to lure better players with bigger paychecks. You can't win the argument on baseball economics.

But isn't this about something more?

——— **Detroit 8 ◇ New York 1** ———

Justin Thompson stifles the world's most expensive lineup.

*8252 Montlieu Street*

Grandma and
Grandpa
Stankiewicz.

As a child I imagined my father's boyhood in black-and-white snippets, like scenes from an *Our Gang* movie. I pieced it together from anecdotes and creased photos and a hundred-odd conversations over many years. It is a childhood that, retold, became an endless streak of baseball games, Saturday matinees, and schoolboy adventures and it always sounded more interesting than my own—filled with characters named Lips and Whitey and Teets and Beezie, and born of a pre-Depression big-city neighborhood that bordered an airport, a cemetery, and a forbidden field by the railroad tracks.

Theodore and Anna Stankiewicz, my grandparents, moved there in 1927 with their brood of children. They had left a home of similar size to escape a painful memory: the death of a daughter. Grandma couldn't bear to live where Dorothy Mae, just a year and some months old, had died. So they got a fresh start on Montlieu Street, which cut through the heart of a scrappy, ten-block working-class area, a place where Stankiewiczes would stay for a half century and be visited by priests, police, and death.

Montlieu was lined with modest two-story wood homes. Most had been built in the mid-1920s by a Mr. Levine, who sold them to factory workers before the stock market crashed and before their jobs disappeared. There were many Poles, to be sure, but also Italians, Germans, Hungarians, Scots, and English—growing families with young children. The homes sat on narrow lots that backed up against alleys. All had porches, some of brick, and front yards small enough to spit a cherry seed over. The houses were so close that when Dad and his brothers peed out the upstairs window they'd hit the Nelsons' place next door.

The Stankiewicz home had a seldom-used front room with two frills: French doors that allowed the space to be shut off—and it was most of the time—and a square-foot window of stained glass that had been imbedded high in the wall, casting a churchlike solemnity on sunny days. Grandma, who went to daily mass, appreciated this feature and complemented it with a framed felt portrait of Christ created by her firstborn, Clem. The portrait, a graduation requirement and a testament to his desire to finish grade school, hung for decades, becoming a quaint embarrassment to Clem when he started keeping company with the aspiring intellectuals, atheists, artists, and writers who called him by his middle name, Max.

The French doors opened into the dining room, where a large oak table dominated the floor space, and a hand-carved cabinet taller than any of the boys stretched toward the high ceiling. But the focus was the radio, often tuned to WWJ and

Ty Tyson's broadcasts of Tiger games. A photo of Grandma's parents, the Tuchewiczes, ruled one wall, a reminder of their very real presence in day-to-day life. Theirs was a serious pose: he with his big walrus moustache and she with her hair pulled tight into a bun, and not a hint of joy on their faces. They lived in Detroit and my grandma was their oldest child of eight. Off the Stankiewicz dining room a small hallway led to the toilet and two bedrooms. One was occupied by daughters Irene and Bernice, the other by Grandma and Grandpa and whichever child qualified for the crib. (Herb, Anna Mae, and Tommy were the last born.) As the boys grew, they ascended to the gabled room upstairs where Clem, Bucky, Teddy, and Joey—my dad—slept.

As in many large families, the kitchen served as the center of activity. It was at the back of the house and looked out on a rose and vegetable garden and the alley beyond. It hosted card games and the petty arguments that sometimes resulted amid the pipe tobacco and yeasty beer. All meals were made and eaten in the kitchen. In good times that might mean boiled pork chops, roasts, and kishka, a blood sausage. Other times it would be vegetable soups and stews, potato pancakes, eggs scrambled with bologna, or pan-fried sandwiches made with thick welfare bread and doctored with whatever you had: bacon grease, onions, tomatoes, ketchup and cheese, or even mustard by itself. The kitchen had yellow walls and a spotty brown linoleum floor that Grandma scrubbed daily before five A.M. Dangling ominously from a hook by the stairs to the second story was a strap with four leather whipping tongues.

Grandma's canned chili sauce, preserves, pickles, and tomatoes were stored in the basement pantry near a tub of apple butter and the beer and root beer that Grandpa bottled. As a teen, Bucky, the second son, had used the pantry door for knife-throwing. Bucky had excellent aim and persuaded his agreeable brother Joey, six years his junior, to stand against the door while he threw blades around Joey's torso, as he'd seen done at the circus. The pantry later doubled as Bucky's photo darkroom. A coal-burning furnace, with arms like an octopus, consumed much of the basement, which also held Grandpa's workbench, where he fixed shoes for neighbors.

In the backyard beside the alley, Grandpa—they called him Pa—planted rose switches that he charmed from local ladies. He nurtured dozens of varieties, but the one that drew the most praise was the Hoover Rose, named for the Republican president. When visitors inquired about its yellow-and-orange petals, Pa, a Democrat, would lie: "Oh, that's the Paderewski Rose." On that block many knew Ignace Jann Paderewski as a Polish hero, a pianist and statesman who had helped his nation gain independence after World War One—a man, in Pa's mind, worthy of the flower's beauty.

By the summer of 1932 the Great Depression had settled over the country. Fifteen million were unemployed, and Detroit, which had boomed through much of the 1920s, became paralyzed. Auto plants closed. Banks failed. Attendance at Tiger games plummeted to about 5,000—less than half of what it had been three years earlier. On Montlieu Street, as everywhere, families struggled to keep their homes and to find food. Pa had been laid off from his job at Chrysler and Bucky had quit school to work at a box factory and contribute to the family. Clem worked, too, but saved his money for New York.

Anna Mae was the ninth Stankiewicz child, a spunky kid with curly blond hair. Like Dorothy Mae before her, she had been given her middle name in honor of the silent-screen actress Mae Busch, one of her ma's favorites. She treasured Bucky, her doting seventeen-year-old brother. Nightly she refused to eat dinner until he returned from work, and then she'd treat him to her abbreviated rendition of "Somebody Loves You," changing the "you" to "me."

That year Anna Mae became ill and the brightness in her eyes dimmed. As always, Ma turned to God (and Dr. Osinski). "Pray to Saint Theresa of the Little Flower," Ma told her. "Offer your suffering up to Saint Theresa." As the spinal meningitis took hold of Anna Mae, Ma sent Bucky to ask a priest to pray that her daughter be relieved of the pain. Anna Mae died at two A.M. on a Sunday morning, shortly after Bucky had returned from a downtown movie house.

The little casket, lined in pink, was set in the front room beyond the French doors. Light from outside streamed through the stained-glass window, touching the casket with hues of red, blue, and gold. Aunties and uncles, cousins and friends, came to the home on Montlieu. A wreath of sorrow hung on the front door. On Ma's dresser was a small crucifix. Anna Mae had liked to remove the nails that held the statue of Christ in place but she could never manage all of them. For weeks after the burial the statue dangled from one nail, just as she had left it.

If such tragedy shook her faith, Ma never let on. She continued her morning walks to mass and insisted on mealtime prayers and blessed her children whenever they left for school or work. In time she came to think of Dorothy and Anna as angels in heaven able to plead the family's case before God.

"Many times we needed the extra help," Clem said later.

One such time involved Teddy who, with a delinquent named Red the Rooster, spotted a parishioner's Packard outside Holy Name Church on a Sunday morning. The keys were still in the ignition. Teddy and Rooster figured they would take the car for a brief ride. Their adventure took a complicated turn when upon returning to the church they found the original parking space occupied. They left the car down the street, hoping no one would be the wiser. Within the hour police were at the Stankiewicz home interrogating Pa about his sons' whereabouts. The younger Teddy confessed. The next day—after a night of fitful praying—he was in court. The judge admonished the Packard owner for leaving the keys visible and came down on The Rooster, who had had previous run-ins with the law; but he took mercy on Teddy, the fifteen-year-old first-time offender. For several years after, when crimes occurred in the neighborhood, police stopped at 8252 Montlieu Street to ask questions.

Teddy wasn't criminally minded, but he stumbled easily and innocently into predicaments.

Once, after Pa had complained of kids stealing apricots from his tree, Teddy stood guard behind the fence and waited. When the thieves appeared, he hammered them with a bat. Days later two local toughs put a noose around his neck and hoisted Teddy into the branches. Only Grandma's knife saved him; she cut him down.

At age eleven Teddy heard his father curse in pain after smacking his knee on the corner of a basement cabinet. "For ten cents, I would chop these down," Pa shouted in Polish. When his parents left the house, Teddy went about the task of putting himself on Pa's good side. He removed and emptied the drawers. He smashed them with an ax. He swung at the side of the beast and then the top of it. Pieces of oak splintered onto the floor. It was hard work but in an hour's time he had transformed the cabinet and its carved front panel into an unrecognizable pile of potential firewood. He waited proudly for Pa to return and greeted him at the door with a demand for money. "You owe me a dime," he said. Pa was baffled by the news but thought it a prank and humored his son. Teddy persisted and Pa headed into the basement with growing concern. His fury erupted. Teddy had expected appreciation, not rage. Ma chalked it up to an honest misunderstanding and calmed her livid husband. Finally Teddy asked again, "Can I have the dime?" Ma insisted Pa pay. Like his father, Teddy had a charming smile, a hawkish nose, and a temper that sparked quickly.

Even in hard times the Stankiewicz boys occasionally found themselves at Navin Field watching the Tigers. Their priest rewarded altar boys with tickets, and the safety patrol went once a year. Police also handed out game passes or looked the other way as youngsters snuck into the gates. Once in a while the boys earned their way into the park as pre-game workers by packing peanuts or sweeping the stands.

The ballpark was eight miles from Montlieu. Getting there involved a series of long walks and streetcar rides. When Teddy went, he had to take Joey. Once out of their mother's sight, Teddy would glare over his left shoulder at his younger brother. "Back up," he demanded. Joey stopped and waited for Teddy and his pal Rich to get half a block ahead. Joey knew better than to anger him. He had once seen Teddy strangle a kid blue after the boy had thrown a handful of dirt in his mouth. Teddy had pounced on him and it took five others to pull him off—otherwise, everyone was convinced, the boy would have died.

In Teddy's view it was bad enough that he had been forced to drag a kid brother to Navin Field; he wasn't about to suffer the degradation of having girls see them walking together. So Joey hung back, trying to dislodge bits of a Mary Jane candy from his teeth. He followed discreetly. Once at the park they sat together in right-center. It looked different then, in the summer of 1934, before being rimmed with a double deck.

Over the winter the Tigers had obtained two Hall of Fame–bound veterans, catcher/manager Mickey Cochrane and outfielder "Goose" Goslin. Both had won World Series: Cochrane with Connie Mack's A's, and Goslin with the Senators. They joined Greenberg and Gehringer, Billy Rogell and Marv Owen, and Arkansas wonder "Schoolboy" Rowe in turning what had been a fifth-place team into the American League's best.

Teddy, Rich, Joey, and a hundred other kids were in those stands that July weekday, imagining themselves on that field. Days earlier, Dad's team had won a city-league title and Jo-Jo White, Detroit's quick-footed center fielder, had presented him a trophy and shaken his hand at Dawn Community Center. It was an honor big enough to make an older brother envious.

Tommy, the youngest, was born in 1934, the tenth child in twenty-one years. Ma was forty and it had been a difficult pregnancy. The doctor was blunt with Pa. "Give her a break," he said. "No more." Ma had spent seven years of her life pregnant. Raising children and keeping house had left her looking perpetually tired. She also handled the money. Pa turned over his check and she gave him an allowance. Perhaps out of necessity, she was his opposite. Outgoing and carefree, he made friends naturally. He sang passionately but not well—"the poor man's Ezio Pinza," Clem said. Pa played cards and extended kindnesses to strangers. He bounced about the neighborhood filled with joy. He could speak English and Polish, of course, but also some German and Russian, which endeared him to a community populated with immigrants. He shared his stemmed roses with the women on the block and his many friends knew him as "good old Teddy."

By comparison Ma was quiet and serious, a bit introverted. She dismissed any praise that came her way, fearing God would question her humility. Though she had little formal education, she enjoyed reading, even tackling Shakespeare, and she could spell flawlessly. Her only frivolous passion was the Big Screen. She loved movies, particularly romances. She'd take in the shows with her daughters or sisters. In those days a visit to the theater might include two features, a variety of shorts, a live comedy act, and free Currier and Ives dishes. She admired Valentino, Douglas Fairbanks, Mary Pickford, Gloria Swanson, John Gilbert, Errol Flynn, Clark Gable, Cary Grant, and the many others who for a few hours would transport her elsewhere. Film was her only escape. In her sixty-nine years she never once spent a night away from home. I've often wondered whether the deaths of two daughters had made her unwilling to venture far from the others.

It certainly affected how she treated my father, for he was a sickly baby. He had jaundice. Because his skin was yellow and they thought he looked Asian, his older brothers called him Choy; eventually "Choy" evolved into "Joy." Well into adulthood, his aunties would pat him on the head—a grown man, as if a child—and tell him, "We didn't think you would make it, Joy." Between the deaths of Dorothy Mae and Anna Mae, my dad was to begin school. But Ma delayed it as long as she could. He started at age eight, never missed a day, passed all grades, and still didn't graduate until he was twenty. Most of the photos from Dad's youth show him in a ball cap or a football helmet or a wool hockey hat, often with a brother or two and a close-knit pack of teens who hung around the home on Montlieu: Castiglione, Glowicki, Konczal, Kahanak, Ritter, Peraino, Curatolo, Supanich. Uncle Bucky took many of the pictures. One captures my dad at fourteen, his head cocked with attitude, a confident smirk on his face. Another has him striding into a pitch. My favorite is set in an alley lined with telephone poles and chicken-wire fences and garbage drums. His back is to the camera, his glove hand outstretched toward a ball tossed by one of his buddies. It's easy to put myself into that photo.

Every family has its stories and its cast of characters. Among the Stankiewiczes, the three eldest sons played starring roles, partly because as adults they best remembered the early days. Clem, Bucky, and Teddy had all arrived within a thirty-five-month period but they grew into young men with diverse interests and outlooks: Clem with his dreams of being a writer, Bucky with his camera and his left-wing passion for the underdog, and Teddy with his sense of adventure and the accepted knowledge that his future lay in a factory.

What they had in common with my dad, aside from Polish blood, was that they loved baseball. Clem, tall and well-proportioned, had a precise and practiced technique that gave him the appearance of a fine athlete. On those good days when he would awaken with his lazy left eye aimed forward rather than away from his nose, he could look as professional as any player on a card. Bucky, who took his nickname from a character in an Edward G. Robinson movie, might have made the big leagues if he hadn't quit school to help support the family. Built like a bulldog, he could drag a bunt down the first-base line and outrun it for a single. Teddy felt such competitiveness that a loss on the diamond would leave him in a foul mood until the next game. Consequently he played for winning teams. My dad may have been the best player among them, though it was up to his brothers to say so. The four of them

My father (*back to camera*) playing catch in the 1930s in the
alley behind Montlieu Street. Photo taken by Uncle Bucky
(Edward Stankiewicz).

spent their summers playing on the diamonds near Montlieu and hatching plans to get into Navin Field to see their Tigers. On Sundays after church, they hung out at semipro fields in Detroit—Northwestern and Belle Isle—watching games with Pa, who would treat them to sodas and candy while he puffed a cigar. The fact that he never played ball didn't keep him from criticizing the athletes. Of a poor hitter who connected for a single, Pa would say, "Even the blind chicken finds the corn once in a while."

**Game 5: Saturday, April 17** ◇ On his pre-game stroll, Ernie Harwell spots George Albano and Steve Hussey behind the Yankee dugout. They've flown in from Norwalk, Connecticut, for the weekend series. They have seen almost four hundred Yankee games together.

"They let you guys back in today?" asks the broadcaster. He recognizes the men from a visit yesterday and it thrills them, for Harwell's name is known throughout baseball, spoken with Red Barber's and Harry Caray's.

"We listened to you last night," says Albano.

"So, you caught two games, the one you saw and the one I announced." A smile crinkles the skin around Harwell's nose.

He wishes the out-of-towners a pleasant game, glances at me as if I'm becoming familiar, and walks off like a man who knows he lives a blessed life.

"There aren't many things that make you feel a couple feet off the ground," says Albano. "But this is one of them."

Rain pelts the diamond in the third inning with the Yankees ahead 1–0. In the rooftop press box, water streaks the long bank of seven-foot windows that look onto the field. Already Paul O'Neill has slipped in right field and catcher Joe Girardi has fallen chasing a ball.

"Hey, what are we doin', waitin' for someone to get hurt?" says a New York reporter, his indignation sounding like a genetic trait. "This is ridiculous."

Writers work at two rows of counters, scoring the game and clicking at their laptops. Those from the largest papers get the higher tier. The rest of us sit below, hunched forward to see the catcher. Which isn't a complaint. This is, after all, a grand place and the hot dogs are free.

I used to dream of being here. In high school, when my fevered delusions of a baseball career snapped like a hard curveball, I turned to writing. It seemed a clever plan. If I couldn't play ball, maybe I could cover it. Every journalism major has a similar story.

At the far end of the arced press booth—the game now delayed by rain—Joe Falls, Detroit's senior sports column-ist, talks on the phone. At seventy-one Falls has a full head of silver-gray hair that contrasts with his bloodred polo shirt. He has mellowed since 1960. That year the Tigers traded batting champion Harvey Kuenn for Cleveland home-run king Rocky Colavito and Falls began tracking an unusual statistic: When Colavito stranded a runner, Falls would give him an RNBI—run *not* batted in. Colavito despised him.

I began reading Falls as a boy. Kids read sports pages to feel closer to their idols. For a long while Willie Horton was mine.

Falls took me beyond the statistics. He told me how Horton, a moody outfielder who grew up in the city's projects, hosted barbecues for his teammates and treated those guys as family. Through Falls I learned that Mickey Lolich drove a motorcycle and that Norm Cash liked to drink and that Al Kaline's dad made brooms.

In time those idols left our playing field. Kaline and Cash retired. Lolich went to the Mets, and Horton to Texas. But Joe Falls kept writing and I kept reading. His column felt like a conversation with a friend. As a teenager I told Falls about my plan to publish a baseball newsletter. He sent me 15 cents for the first issue.

"A writer can always use money," he said.

You never forget your heroes and this ballpark is filled with them.

—— **Detroit 3** ◇ **New York 1** ——

After two rain delays, the Tigers rally in the late innings.

**Game 6: Sunday, April 18** ◇ On the concourse above the first-base stands—not far from where Paws, the team mascot, high-fives children—hot-dog vendor Art Witkosky watches the game. It's the fifth inning and Dave Mlicki, obtained in a trade with Los Angeles two days ago, has held the Yankees to four hits and one run. "We might just win all three," Art says.

Still in his blue-and-red uniform—his folded pant legs revealing Nikes scuffed like a cue ball—he leans against a steel beam, his working day done. He sold 320 dogs today and his arms and legs are tired from lugging the vending case.

"It feels like a hundred pounds," he says.

Art, in his seventies, says he could lessen his load and make twice the money by hawking pretzels or popcorn. "But I've been selling dogs for twenty-seven years. It's what I'm known for and I've got many regulars who look for me. They remember me from their childhood."

Some vendors draw attention by growling their sales lines, by singing, by yelling. Not Art. He works the prime area between first and third, close to the field. He sets his case on an empty seat, tosses a bag of buns high into the air, and waits for customers to call out, raise their hands, or make eye contact. Then he skips up the aisle with dogs in hand, or on request wraps them in a plastic bag and throws them to the buyer.

"I can go through a whole game without saying a word."

Despite his relative silence, Art is the park's most-recognized vendor. He is a roving photo opportunity. For starters there's the white hair. White, not gray. Next, the ice cream–man smile. Then the stop-action poses: Art doffing his cap, Art hoisting the buns, Art confirming the number of dogs by raising his fingers.

"I always liked baseball as a kid," he says. "Played in the streets not far from here. First game was a twelve-year-old in '38. Came to the park as a safety-patrol boy."

Art refers to vending as his "full-time part-time job." In the off-season he and his wife travel. Mexico. France. Belgium.

Sell pretzels for more money? Nah. It's not about money anymore.

—— **Detroit 5** ◇ **New York 1** ——

Tony Clark brings in four runs and the Tigers sweep the champs.

**Game 7: Tuesday, April 20** ◇ Several days have passed since the Tigers took outdoor batting practice. The field has been wet and the team confined to a snug hitting room beneath the left-center stands. Today it is bright and dry and the mood is warm as Al Kaline, sixty-four, approaches the cage, graceful still.

Trim and graying, Kaline is as much a part of this park as anyone. He arrived in 1953, months out of high school, never having played in the minor leagues. He looked so young that a guard refused to let him in the gate when he reported for his first day. From outside, the park reminded Kaline of a battleship.

In his second full season he won the American League hitting title, at age twenty the youngest man to do it. For that summer and many to follow, he was an All-Star on a team that rarely contended. When the club finally made it to the World Series in 1968 Detroiters rooted for a win; not only for themselves, deprived of a Series appearance since 1945, or for the city, shattered by race riots—but for Al Kaline who had played sixteen sterling seasons with dignity, decency, and loyalty, and who at age thirty-three might not get a second chance. Kaline hit .379 and the Tigers won the championship. It was his only World Series.

In the 1960s and early 1970s we Michigan boys aspired to be Al Kaline. On dusty schoolyard fields in neighborhood pickup games, we called out first to claim his name, leaving others with Cash, Freehan, and Horton, honorable second choices. We emulated his stance: upright, balanced, front shoulder back, back elbow up, not too high. He was such a part of our lives that we thought alkaline batteries had been named in his honor.

Like Yastrzemski in Boston and Clemente in Pittsburgh, like Ernie Banks in Chicago and Brooks Robinson in Baltimore, Al Kaline spent his Hall of Fame career with one team, our team. He remains the closest thing we have to a baseball saint, the antithesis of Ty Cobb.

Most guys on this year's club never saw Kaline play; some weren't born when he retired. They know him, of course, and they see his uniform number—6—hanging along the facing of the roof, where it belongs, above the position he mastered, right field.

"Cat Man, how you doing?" asks Kaline at the batting cage.

"Mister K," responds Frank Catalanotto, a twenty-four-year-old infielder.

Kaline pats Tony Clark on the rear and lays an arm across the shoulders of Juan Encarnacion, an outfielder from the Dominican Republic.

"Ah, you're just a babe," he says.

The players draw near Kaline as if he were the fire on a cold night.

I want to ask him why he's here. He's not scheduled to broadcast. He's not coaching. Has he shown up, serendipitously, on this park's birthday?

April 20, 1912—the day should be trumpeted. There should be balloons and bunting. A celebration. A cake. There is none of that. Just silence. They would prefer we forget.

It opened in the era of ragtime music and black Model T's. Airplanes were still aeroplanes, Mary Pickford was becoming a star, and Jim Thorpe soon would be. The First World War had yet to begin and women wouldn't get the right to vote for eight years. It was a time when fans wore sports coats and dress hats and paid to stand in the outfield, separated from the players not by a home-run fence but by a rope that defined the playing area.

Frank Navin, who ran the club and owned it with Bill Yawkey, had admired the new parks in Philadelphia, St. Louis, and Pittsburgh and wanted to build one in Detroit that reflected the city's growing prosperity and the team's status as home to the sport's biggest drawing card, Ty Cobb. In the fall of 1911 after Cobb, twenty-four, hit .420 and led the league for the fifth straight season, Navin knocked down the wooden stands of fifteen-year-old Bennett Park and constructed a cement-and-steel structure that would become the foundation of today's Tiger Stadium. The field, like Fenway in Boston, was to be introduced on a Thursday—April 18—but it rained that day in both cities. Navin, a superstitious poker player and horse-race gambler, decided against a Friday debut and settled on Saturday for the first game.

Ironically, tonight Detroit plays Boston, which inaugurated its park on this date, too. Since the 1990 demise of Comiskey in Chicago, Fenway and Tiger Stadium have held distinction as the oldest ball fields. Next year the honor will fall to Fenway alone.

I want to believe that Kaline knows the significance of today. Yet I cannot ask him. In my journalism career I've talked to Elton John, been in the company of Hillary Rodham Clinton, and made conversation with Mike Wallace. But it is Al Kaline who makes me most nervous.

He is behind the batting cage now with Alan Trammell. They and Cobb are the only players to have spent twenty years in a Tiger uniform. As they chat I hear a familiar tinny sound, like the rustling of car keys.

It's Kaline and he's jangling the coins in his pocket, just like my dad.

—— **Boston 1** ◇ **Detroit 0** ——

Pedro Martinez wins the pitching duel against Jeff Weaver, whom teammates have begun to call Roy, short for "Rookie of the Year."

**Game 8: Wednesday, April 21** ◇ A boy about seven stands next to his dad at a tub-shaped urinal. He stretches to pee into the trough, like the bigger guys scattered about the room.

"You're a man now," his dad says.

A few laugh.

For kids accustomed to post–World War Two toilets, the first visit to the facilities at Tiger Stadium can feel like a rite of passage.

It is what I remember most of a Saturday trip in June 1971. Our St. Malachy coaches had brought us downtown to celebrate a winning season in the ten-and-under league. Late in the game, Tony, our stuttering right fielder, began squirming, his belly full of Coke.

"I've gggg-gggg-ggotta pee," he said.

Our coach herded us into a crowded men's room where hung a pungent odor, a blend of urine and cigar smoke. With the stalls full and others waiting, Tony and I stepped up for our public unveiling. We angled our bodies for privacy, each catching a discreet look at the other's and at the late entry, that of Chris's dad.

Tony and I stared at the porcelain, watching our spent sodas swirl toward the drain, yellow as a cheap Chinese chicken broth.

We left the restroom as men.

—— **Detroit 9** ◇ **Boston 2** ——

Dean Palmer belts two homers, driving in five runs.

**Game 9: Thursday, April 22** ◇ It started in the 1970s when a friend showed Steve Olsen how to score a ball game.

"I've gotten to this point where it's almost overkill," he says.

Olsen tracks every game he attends, recording each play as it occurs. He uses a precisely lined scoresheet that he made on his computer. He prints the scoresheet on card stock so it doesn't flip in the wind. He uses goldenrod stock, not white, to mute the glare of the sun. He includes an alphabetized key to his twenty-two abbreviations (AT for "advanced on throw," AU for "advanced unopposed," BK for "balk," and on and on).

The day after the contest, Olsen, fifty-three, reconciles his account with the official version in the newspaper. He transfers the entire game to another scoresheet, attaching league standings, team averages, and a box score to the reverse side. Finally he punches holes into the sheet and places it in a binder containing seven years' worth of such records.

"What I've developed here is a system of code that I can understand that other people—casual fans—can't," he says. "I can go back years and relive a game."

In his meticulosity Olsen reminds me of my uncle Teddy, who worked weekends as an official scorer for the Federation League. Though he got paid, he would have done it for free. He simply liked being part of the game and he liked documenting the details of life. (He kept a log of every movie he saw, every book he read, and every hit he earned; after he died, a relative sold it at a garage sale.) The fact that Teddy and Aunt Sadie could not have children and that his Chrysler job rarely occupied his Saturdays or Sundays meant that he could spend hours at amateur games.

Unlike most of his brothers, Teddy stayed in Detroit. When

Dad and I went to games with him, we'd pick him up and park in the Corktown neighborhood across Michigan Avenue, on the lawn of a chain-smoking woman who charged a buck or two and pledged to watch our '72 Nova until we returned. It was 1975 and I was fourteen when I finally scrutinized Uncle Teddy's scoring system. He used horizontal slashes to indicate hits—one slash for a single, two for a double—and he circled the slashes if the batter scored.

Uncle Teddy loved the sport. He had played ball while stationed in Australia in the 1940s. He was an excellent pitcher who had bowel problems. Because the soldiers gambled on the games, they went to the unusual length of building him a makeshift toilet that he could visit between innings. Into his sixties he continued to play softball, a chattering catcher in the mold of Birdie Tebbetts.

Unlike my uncle, Steve Olsen came to baseball in his late twenties. He was a native of Alabama. "I didn't grow up in this park and I don't get tingly all over and remember Ty Cobb," he says. "I remember the good times, the funny things that have happened, and the strangers I've met. You can have a good time with anyone." Which is fortunate for Olsen because his wife and adult children rarely accompany him.

In the eighth inning when Brad Ausmus homers for the Tigers, Olsen draws a diamond on his scorecard and shades it. He puts a nine in the lower left corner, signifying the ball was hit to right field. Meanwhile fans head for their cars.

"People who leave early drive me crazy," he says.

A ninth of the way into this season, I've been surprised by the pleasure I find in other fans, people as quirky as myself who love baseball. You can spot them. Often they come alone or in pairs, with homemade sandwiches or a stick of beef jerky from the corner store. They feel drawn to the park, and I to them.

Recently I dug out that 1975 scorebook. From my uncle's draftsmanlike print I can tell that in the fifth inning Cookie Rojas got to first on an error by Aurelio Rodriguez, advanced to second on a hit by Fran Healy, and scored when Freddie Patek singled. All of that information is contained in a space no bigger than a child's fingernail. The sheet also shows that Kansas City beat us 10–5. What it doesn't show is that after Ron LeFlore got his second triple, Uncle Teddy started laughing in his hiccupy sort of way. It also doesn't show that we had a great time. I guess that's understood.

—— **Detroit 1** ◇ **Boston 0** ——

Justin Thompson two-hits the Sox. Todd Jones picks up his one-hundredth career save.

## ◇ ◇ ◇ ◇ ◇ ◇   *The Corner*

Briggs Stadium, 1940s. Photo courtesy of Burton
Historical Collection, Detroit Public Library.

**Game 10: Tuesday, May 4** ◇ Every killing has a
killer, even that of a ballpark.

On this, the first beautiful day of the season, John McHale
Jr., the team president, has abandoned one layer of formality,
his suit coat. Still, with a white, cuff-linked shirt and hand-
knotted bow tie, he looks starched, alone near the dugout with
uniformed ushers talking in the background and players prac-
ticing before him. The gates haven't opened and McHale, fifty,
can watch peacefully, maybe for the joy of it, as he might have
when his father, a former first baseman, became general manager in 1957. Thirty-four years later the younger McHale, an
ex–Notre Dame linebacker, entered baseball as an executive

with the Colorado Rockies. In 1995 he returned to the city of his birth to help the Tigers build a contender and a stadium. One of the two is on schedule.

As a kid I could identify a bad guy. At movies it was the snarling, black-Stetsoned gunman at whom John Wayne aimed his eyes; in war, the Russians; in politics, Nixon. The worst was Eric, the bully of our block who spit on my best friend and stoned us as we rode past his house. We loved to hate Eric.

There is pleasure in despising one who earns it.

As an adult, identifying the target is sometimes more complicated. As much as I want to blame somebody for the loss of this ballpark, I can't blame John McHale Jr. This place is dying at the hands of many people.

We could start with the owner, Mike Ilitch; ultimately, he decided. Yet if he hadn't bought the team in 1992, his predecessor Tom Monaghan would have left the park. Monaghan and president Bo Schembechler made good villains, defending the firing of Ernie Harwell and threatening to move the club out of Michigan. It was fun to hate them. They're gone, though, and Ilitch has been smarter. Before them, the quiet John Fetzer owned the team. He dreamed of a domed stadium. My 1972 yearbook with the stained Mickey Lolich cover has pictures of the model.

"Ah, there's nothing wrong with the one we got," my dad said back then, and I agreed.

In truth, a gang of a million has killed Tiger Stadium: from owners to players, to mayors, to voters, to the fans who didn't come, to the New York Yankees, to the free-agent system that has made every athlete a lottery winner, and on and on.

It's tough to maintain robust anger when you're uncertain whom specifically you're angry with. It's even tougher when it's 76 degrees on a spring day and you feel the hardness melting like ice in August and you wish you were on the field with the ballplayers, joshing one another and taking cuts in the batting cage.

—— Detroit 3 ◇ Anaheim 1 ——

Dean Palmer's two-run homer into the overhang gives reliever Doug Brocail the win. While on an eleven-game road trip, the Tigers traded Brian Hunter to make room for rookie Gabe Kapler.

**Game 11: Wednesday, May 5** ◇ They tell us the new place will have much that Tiger Stadium doesn't. There will be a merry-go-round, a cigar bar, and a dancing-water show. But with an outfield open to the skyline, it will lack the one feature that has distinguished this park since the 1930s.

Baseball gives designers the freedom to make quirky fields. It's unlike other sports. In the NFL one hundred yards separate the end zones wherever the game is played. In pro basketball and hockey the size of the surface never changes.

Outfields vary in baseball. A ball hit 405 feet to straightaway center will be a home run at Baltimore's Camden Yards. In Denver at Coors Field, it will fall a few yards short of the fence. Some outfield walls are six feet high. Fenway's Green Monster is four stories, and the wall at Chicago's Wrigley is covered with ivy.

In Detroit the upper deck in right juts ten feet over the field, like a long theater balcony. It stretches from foul line to dead center and snags fly balls that might otherwise be outs. A ball driven 320 feet on a line can be caught. One lifted high and descending at the 315-foot mark will fall into the overhang for a home run. The outfielder will be looking up at the underbelly of the deck, waiting beneath the eaves for a ball that has been snatched from the sky.

At the replacement venue, Comerica Park—named for a bank—there will be dozens of diversions for people bored by the sport. And no overhang.

On the field today Jeff Weaver, twenty-two, plays catch in left, loosening his arm before his fifth major-league start. Slender and tall, he looks like a praying mantis when he brings his left leg up. He's won three of four games. He represents the future. Across the field is the future past, Joe Coleman, fifty-two, and hardly anyone recognizes him now.

—— **Anaheim 4** ◇ **Detroit 1** ——

Jeff Weaver gives up three hits, one a home run to Mo Vaughn.

**Game 12: Thursday, May 6** ◇ At home in an upstairs closet in my son's room, I keep boxes of baseball cards. If you look through them you'll find a 1971 Topps, with a nicked black border, of twenty-four-year-old Joe Coleman, who came here in the Denny McLain trade. In our neighborhood, with its smooth streets and maple saplings, you wouldn't trade a Coleman card for a Hank Aaron.

Coleman had a future and for three years he lived up to it, winning sixty-two games from 1971 to 1973. At twenty-six he had his best season, twenty-three victories.

"I really enjoyed playing here," he says before the game, his face puffy and red, a cold sore on his lip. "The fans in those days were tremendous. We had good players and a good ballpark. When I was traded in '76, I really didn't want to go but I was struggling."

A bullpen coach, Coleman stands along the foul line waiting for Anaheim starter Chuck Finley, whose warm-up he will oversee. He looks up at the overhang and then pans to the right. "Anaheim refurbished its park beautifully," he says. "I don't know if there's more they could have done here. Who knows, if maybe they had taken care of it better."

Every kid who loves baseball reaches an age where the coaches' names become as familiar as the players'. The stars of yesterday stay in the sport because there are few things they know better. Rod Carew, Jim Rice, Larry Bowa, Chris Chambliss, Bucky Dent, Frank Howard—they once played in All-Star games. Now they hang out by the batting cage or hit grounders or flash signals from the coach's box.

When I was eleven and hovering near the dugout for autographs, my dad pointed to a coach in a Brewer uniform.

"Ask him," he said.

The guy signed and I showed Dad the ball. "Who's that?"

"Harvey Kuenn," he said. "One of the best Tiger shortstops ever."

That ball is in the upstairs closet, too.

—— **Detroit 4 ◇ Anaheim 2** ——

Gabe Kapler hits his first Tiger Stadium home run.

**Game 13: Friday, May 7** ◇ For their seventh anniversary, Mike Lewis got his wife Tina tickets to a ball game.

"He brought me to see another man," she says.

The other man is older with short hair that grays at the temples and disappears around the crown. He wears the Orioles' number 8, and on this sunny day in the breeze most eyes watch as he scoops grounders at third and throws sidearm to second, a black batting glove hanging from his rear pocket.

Cal Ripken Jr. draws crowds wherever he goes. It's been this way since 1995, when Ripken broke Lou Gehrig's record for consecutive games played. Mike and Tina Lewis were in bed with the game on and she grew to love Ripken. For almost seventeen seasons he started every game: 2,632 in a row. Tonight he won't play due to a nerve irritation in his back.

"I'm just glad to be this close to him," she says.

Mike Conrad and John Mihaljevic have seen Ripken too many times to count. Conrad lives near Baltimore, frequents Camden Yards, and wears an Orioles cap. Mihaljevic has on a Ripken jersey. They're in their early thirties and on another of their baseball journeys, this one to five parks in four days. In January Mihaljevic gets all of the major- and minor-league schedules and begins planning. "I had to ask my boss for an extra week of vacation because I scheduled too many games," he says.

"We have no lives," adds Conrad, laughing.

Both wanted to visit Tiger Stadium this year.

"It's nice to be where Ty Cobb and Babe Ruth played," says Mihaljevic. He looks out at the field and then up at the girders rusting at the joints. "You can see why they're replacing it."

Actually, I can see peeling paint and chipped cement and posts that block views and they don't bother me. I also like baseball cards with corners smoothed from handling and yard-sale scorebooks with fevered markings.

"Camden Yards is great," notes Conrad, "but it has no history."

"This is somewhere we had to be before it disappeared," adds Mihaljevic. "Michigan and Trumbull is the most famous address in baseball."

Outside the park prior to the game, the two did what thousands have done before them. Conrad snapped Mihaljevic's photo across from the main gates by the green-and-white street signs that identify the celebrated intersecting avenues, a spot known simply as The Corner; the sport has been played here since the 1896 opening of Bennett Park. But the history of the locale, of course, predates professional baseball.

William Woodbridge, secretary of the Michigan Territory, owned the land in the early 1800s and it remained in his family long after he had served as governor. He named Trumbull Avenue for his father-in-law, writer John Trumbull, author of *M'Fingal*, a mock epic published during the American Revolution. Trumbull, who studied law under John Adams and was a friend of Noah Webster, retired to Detroit after serving on the Connecticut high court. He died in 1831. Twenty years later the corner lot became a public picnic area, Woodbridge Grove, and then, around 1875, Western Market, where bales of hay were sold next to the DeMan Brothers' planing mill. Both roads were dirt.

The intersection took on greater significance with the construction of Bennett Park. Home plate was where right field is today. When "Wild Bill" Donovan pitched to Nap Lajoie and "Wee Willie" Keeler, he threw toward Trumbull and Michigan, backed by outfield walls with ads for Stroh's beer, Goodyear raincoats, and Beeman's Pepsin Gum. In 1912 Navin Field replaced Bennett and the site's prominence was ensured. Though home plate moved to what had been left field—to keep the setting sun out of batters' eyes—the main entrance remained on Trumbull Avenue, a quarter block from Michigan, steps from a streetcar stop. The entrance, which included the ticket office, was Spanish-inspired with a tiled roof and rounded gables, and it stood through the thirties and forties, even as the ballpark itself grew and its name changed. In the 1950s a block building succeeded it and an advance-ticket booth rose close to the intersection. Behind it was the players' parking lot, shielded by green walls. The lot was replaced in 1993 by the Tiger Plaza, a decoratively fenced, open-air court which gave The Corner its current look.

On game days as start time approaches, pedestrians crowd sidewalks near the intersection, waiting for traffic cops to wave them through. They spill across Michigan Avenue's nine lanes, across the red-brick road striped with a center band of asphalt where tracks once ran. Some head straight for the turnstiles, set tight, one next to the other, each with a ticket taker on the other side. Some come early and have burgers and beer at ordinary neighborhood bars like Reedy's or Hoot Robinson's or Shelley's Place, opposite the gates, or at the more stylish Nemo's, a few blocks down Michigan Avenue. Some stop at souvenir shops with names like Designated Hatter or Sportsland USA, or to buy peanuts from vendors who work the corners. Many pause to read the bronze plaque of Ty Cobb—"a genius in spikes"—anchored to the stadium. Another sign proclaims the park a historic site. Across the street is the three-story Checker Cab building; it was here when my dad came as a boy. And further down is Brooks Lumber, still owned by the Brooks family, who contributed to the original Bennett Park. Farther yet is the expressway.

Though the neighborhood comes alive on game days, it is not an area that otherwise draws people. Within a block you will find boarded-up buildings and weed-infested property. You would not ordinarily walk these streets at night. The houses that once abutted the stadium disappeared long ago to make room for parking. Nearby in Corktown, an area settled by Irish fleeing the potato famine, there are signs of resurgence in homes with fresh paint and neat lawns and maybe a bed-and-breakfast. But mostly there is one reason to come to Michigan and Trumbull: the ballpark. It's gray-sided now, its top trimmed in blue. The back of the upper deck in right still bulges out above the sidewalk, as if the building can barely contain what's happening inside. And that is the telltale sign, for what is most special about this celebrated intersection is what takes place inside the building that has in one shape or another occupied The Corner for most of a century.

—— **Baltimore 9 ◇ Detroit 4** ——

Justin Thompson surrenders seven runs in less than four innings.

**Game 14: Saturday, May 8** ◇ I wanted Mike Varney to get a look at this seat because he appreciates such things. It's perched over foul territory on the edge of right field, a corner seat in the front row of the upper deck with a view that puts baseball on two sides, before you and to your right.

"This is a great place to watch a game," he says.

During batting practice as we're standing in the sun admiring the view, Harold Baines drives a ball between us. It bullets off a seat in the next row and Mike pounces on it.

The ball arrived the same way Mike did in 1983 when he came into my newspaper office, unexpected, uninvited, a twenty-nine-year-old Air Force officer so cheerful in volunteering as a sports writer that my business partner suspected he was a spy from the weekly down the street. A doctoral intern, Mike looked like the bespectacled "Ernie" from *My Three Sons* all grown up: short, starting to bald, and imbued with an optimism that could startle.

I didn't suspect that he would change my life—not in shades of beige, as everyone we meet changes us, but boldly.

Mike and Georgia, his British wife, left two years later for an assignment in England. The letters, though not frequent, came regularly in tiny block print, long and thoughtful letters about politics and lofty ideals and his daily discoveries in Oxford and Oslo; two or three letters a year over seven years, with an occasional phone call telling of the birth of their two children and celebrating the birth of our three. When the Air Force finally brought them Stateside, we made the journeys to their homes in the Midwest and they to ours. I believe you can measure the depth of friendship by the volume of silence it can absorb in comfort. With Mike shared silence never feels awkward.

He grew up in rural Wisconsin, playing Pee Wee ball in a league where kids ran teams and made lineups. Once a year his dad Sonny would drive Mike and his older brother three and a half hours to watch Hank Aaron and the Braves. It was their tradition until the team moved to Atlanta in 1966.

"When the Braves left Milwaukee, part of me died," says Mike, who was twelve at the time. "I felt abandoned and betrayed. Suddenly spring came and there were no Braves games on the radio or TV. They just disappeared. I stopped following the players: Aaron, Eddie Mathews, Joe Torre, Woody Woodward, Rico Carty. When you're a traitor, you're a traitor."

By the time baseball returned to Milwaukee in the early seventies, much had changed. The Beatles were singing of "The Long and Winding Road," anti-war protestors were rallying in Washington, and students were dying at Kent State. Mike had learned to drive and begun dating. But the Brewers weren't the Braves and baseball wasn't the same. Maybe it never is once we leave the summers of childhood.

Some time later a drunk driver hit Mike head-on. The crash occurred on the edge of the Mohave Desert in a sandstorm.

"Right before impact I leaned to the right," he says. "That saved me from getting crushed by the steering wheel. I must have been knocked out for a bit. The only thing I can remember is thinking, 'I want to live.' I have always wondered if I had told myself, 'I am dead,' would I have been? Is that how it happens?"

I think that Mike's brush with death made him the type of man who will on a moment's notice drive hours out of his way to honor the white stripes on an empty Big Ten football field or to admire the encrusted gargoyles atop a city library or to check out a neighborhood bar that a friend mentioned. He follows his heart. It's a quality that has its charm.

In January as Wisconsin rose from a blizzard, we sipped coffee at a beanery that looked out on a snowy Milwaukee streetscape and shoveled through our dreams for the coming year, as we do each winter. I rambled through a list of possibilities as chaotic as notes on a bar napkin.

"Maybe I'll go to every game of the final season."

"That's it," he said. "The other things will wait."

And so began this mission.

Mike's words can resonate with me in ways he never intended.

"People can create their own heaven or their own hell," he says today after having driven 353 miles to this game. "Life's short."

Though he's not referring to me, I recognize myself. A month ago I set out to answer questions about my attachment to this ballpark. In truth I have been creating a hell of sorts, tainting these days with anger. Some of it you may have detected; some has been swallowed only to eat at my insides. It—my anger—is the enemy.

—— **Detroit 7** ◇ **Baltimore 6** ——

Bobby Higginson leaps above the right-field wall, depriving the Orioles of the tying run. The win leaves the Tigers one game under .500.

**Game 15: Sunday, May 9** ◇ On Mother's Day it's cold in the shade.

"I was going to bring a hat and gloves but I thought I'd look like a nut," says Beth, my wife. "Instead I am sitting here with a sweater on my head."

Still, that's nothing compared to Gabe Kapler's humiliation. After he makes a diving catch that saves a run, the scoreboard blinks in celebration: *Kappy! Kappy! Kappy!* With his muscles, modeling credentials—he's a fitness-magazine cover boy— and Hollywood childhood, Gabe deserves a more colorful name. "Kappy" conjures a grizzled sailor with smooth gums and caterpillar brows. When Kirk Gibson played right field they called him "Gibby." Bobby Higginson became "Higgy." And now Kapler appears doomed to carry on this mundane tradition. I suppose if Kaline were a rookie they'd call him "Kally." They should know that the best nicknames come from fans, not marketing departments.

This afternoon our three sons are trying to score the game, biding time with hot dogs and Cokes until after the contest when they, like any child here, can step onto this legendary field and run the bases with their mom. But when the time comes, no one runs. They walk, and my boys collect grass and pebbles along the way.

I tell them another story they should remember, about how in the late 1920s their great-uncle Bucky, whom they cherish, picked stones from this infield and earned himself a free admission to Mr. Navin's park, and how as a teen he played a scrimmage on this hallowed turf, taking center field like Harry Heilmann, one of his favorites, and how he once saw Lou Gehrig hit the scoreboard in left five times during a double-header.

"That was in the days of Charlie Gehringer," I begin. "He was a real quiet second baseman but one of the best ever. He never bragged, just did his job. Sort of like Grandpa Joe. Some people called Gehringer the Mechanical Man because he was so dependable. But Grandpa says he fielded too smoothly to be mechanical. That's Gehringer's uniform number up there."

They look at the number 2 on the third deck.

"In those days, players didn't make much money. In the winter a lot of them had other jobs. Charlie Gehringer worked at Hudson's, which used to be downtown. Can you imagine Bobby Higginson selling cars in the off-season? Gehringer was Grandpa Joe's favorite player and he hardly ever swung at the first pitch . . ."

—— **Baltimore 5** ◇ **Detroit 0** ——

Cal Ripken Jr. doesn't play in the series.

◇ ◇ ◇ ◇ ◇ ◇ ◇   *Dad's Regrets*

Uncle Ted,
Uncle Tom,
Dad, and a
friend.

**Game 16: Tuesday, May 11** ◇ It's 72 degrees this
evening and the Oakland pitchers do not want to be confined
to the cramped, sunken bullpen near the right-field foul line.
So they sit on benches outside the pen, their backs against the
front-row railing directly before the fans. Tonight that means
they must endure a college kid who wants to implicate himself
into their lives. From the front row he bends toward them,
dropping their first names into his sentences and whispering
wicked asides as if they're his fraternity brothers. At first
some answer politely. But when he persists, they lean away,
his ignored comments growing into a stageless soliloquy. He
gulps his beer and intrudes further by resting his crossed legs

behind their heads. One by one they drift into the bullpen or down the bench near a guy in his late twenties who taunts the ball boy.

"Run, chubby, run," the guy hollers, turning to see if we're impressed.

The ball boy, seventeen-year-old Adam Ochmanek, plays tackle for the Divine Child football team. He can't say a word. Tiger policy mandates that he not respond.

I can but don't. I am like my father in that respect. Rather than confront, we walk away, our objections unspoken, our offenders unaware. I wonder sometimes if that same trait led Dad's younger brothers, Herb and Tommy, to fade from our lives like faces on a Polaroid.

It seems unlikely with Herb. He was the most combative of the Stankiewicz children—and not by default. None of the boys was timid and Bucky especially was a powerful presence. But while Bucky exerted his strength to maintain order or protect siblings, Herb was indiscriminate. He enjoyed confrontation. It started early, with a disdain for rules. At Holy Name School he broke the silence in Sister Catherine Joseph's class by humming loudly whenever she spoke. Pa dealt with his son's disobedience, as he usually did, with force. In time Herb learned to escape Pa's beatings. He could outrun his father, a man by then in his mid-fifties. He darted from room to room and around tables and over chairs. He skittered under the bed, latched on to the springs, and lifted himself off the floor. Pa's flailing arms and Ma's words could not reach him.

One day in 1941, Herb, fourteen, pulled up to the dinner table on Montlieu Street, struck a match, and lit a cigarette. Before anyone said a word, he announced, pointing his right index finger for effect, "I won't smoke in the house if you don't want me to. But I am smoking and I ain't gonna run around and do it behind your back. I ain't gonna hide like the rest of 'em." He crushed the cigarette on his plate and left the table. If Bucky, the enforcer, had been home, he would have pounced upon him for disrespecting their mother. But Bucky, who was thirteen years older and often the only one able to keep Herb in line, had been drafted into the service.

Of the eight Stankiewicz children who survived to adulthood, the first six came no more than two to three years apart. The last two, Herb and Tommy, were separated by seven years, which meant that when Tommy was seven and Herb was fourteen their brothers were already men of twenty-one, twenty-five, twenty-seven, and twenty-eight. Tommy and Herb lived distinct childhoods. Once able to roam, Herb spent little time on Montlieu. He liked to drink and party. He dressed in zoot suits with long jackets, padded shoulders, and pants that puffed at the knees, just below the fighting chains that draped to his thigh. In neighborhood bars Herb positioned himself strategically with his back to the wall and all potential enemies before him. He took on— and beat—three men in a single fight. Short and compact, Herb commanded fear. When he gave orders, his friends jumped.

"You're bigger than him. Why do you listen to him?" my dad asked one of Herb's pals.

"Have you ever said no to your brother?" the young man responded.

Herb had a sarcastic edge that could alienate people. He had a habit of asking a question and then rapidly snapping his fingers as if the answer were too slow. Upon meeting my mother he had surveyed her slender figure and remarked, "I've seen better legs on a piano." She never forgot it.

In the dark hours of early morning on Tuesday, March 30, 1943, my grandma awoke to the cries of her son Bucky. In her sleep she heard his anguished voice calling from across an ocean. He was in North Africa and she knew that he had been injured. Daughter Bernice found her in the kitchen, rocking in a chair, saying a rosary. Pa was still at the Chrysler plant, having volunteered for the midnight shift so one of the new female laborers could work days.

That morning after getting her youngest ready for school, Ma headed out the door, past the four white stars that hung in her windows, one for each of her soldier sons. She walked up Montlieu in a black babushka beneath the bare elms to Gilbo, and then on Gilbo to Nuernberg past other houses with stars of their own to Holy Name Church, where at seven A.M. Father Louis delivered the early mass and Ma prayed to Saint Anne.

Days passed, maybe a week or more, before she got the telegram confirming that Bucky was in the hospital. He had been hit by shrapnel from a scatter bomb. Though painful, the injury was not life-threatening. He would dance again.

Of her sons, Bucky had been drafted first, followed by Joey, then Teddy and Clem. They made Pa proud and they made Ma worry, causing her to lose seventy pounds. She had hoped to keep her boys out of service, offering that Clem's eyes were poor and that Bucky had high blood pressure and that Teddy suffered from bad nerves and that Joey was too soft and that Herb—who would soon be volunteering—was too young. Still, four of them ended up overseas and all of them came home.

My dad was the luckiest, stationed in St. Joseph, Missouri, where in a club one night he spotted Betty Muse, a shapely brunette with bouncy hair and violet eyes and a sassy-enough smile that he felt he could ask her, "Would you like to dance or would you prefer to sit on my lap?" In 1944 he brought her home, taking the train to the grand Michigan Central Depot, blocks from Briggs Stadium. "Prince Hal" Newhouser, the sandlot star against whom my dad had gotten those two hits, was in his fifth season with the Tigers, on his way to twenty-nine victories. But they didn't see a game.

Instead she met his parents, his sisters, and his ten-year-old brother Tommy. Betty was neither Catholic nor Polish. If they were bothered by that, they didn't mention it in the front room near the stained-glass window by the photos of their six sons in uniform—five in military dress, Tommy in his Scouting outfit.

After World War Two Herb made a career of the military. Serving in Korea he met and married a local woman, TuRan, who died in the 1980s. We've not seen him since Lyndon Johnson was president. The last Christmas card came seven or eight years ago. My dad wonders if he is alive.

It was different with Tommy, whose war experience was limited to bottle-cap battles in vacant parking lots. He and Dad possessed similar soft hearts and sweet natures and they felt a true bond. Home on leave from Rosecrans Field, Dad would always make time for his little brother. Tommy loved baseball and they played catch in the alley behind Pa's rose-bushes. They canoed at Belle Isle, the park designed by Frederick Law Olmsted, and they may even have come to Briggs Stadium—Dad can't remember for sure. I have a photo of them in front of the home on Montlieu. Dad is in his pressed Air Corps uniform, cap on straight, tie crisply knotted. He is crouched down with a niece balanced on one knee, a nephew leaning on his left shoulder, and Tommy to his right, standing straight as a soldier. Tommy has on a sport coat, probably home-sewn, with all three buttons fastened, and pants two inches too short. His dark hair curls onto his forehead from beneath a snap-brim hat and he looks as if he couldn't be happier. In the porch window behind them, the faint outline of a starred flag appears.

Tommy was a good student and became the only of Theodore and Anna Stankiewicz's children to attend college.

As such he brought pride to the family. His oldest brothers helped Pa pay for his education. Tommy became an engineer, working on the Redstone Missile project. He lavished gifts on nephews and nieces and took us to parks and on picnics as Dad once did with him. It is a sign of how close they were that Dad named me in Tommy's honor.

Early in adulthood Tommy lived on Montlieu and took his ma for Sunday drives in the country.

"He was very good to her. After my father passed away in '57, my mother would come over with Tom," Dad says. "He'd bring her once a week. When she was ready to leave, he'd go to the car first and she would always say to me, 'I know you will but I want you to watch over your brother when I'm gone.' She used to say that every time. I used to say, 'You're not going anyplace. What are you talking about?' She'd say, 'You've got to promise that you're going to watch him.' I promised."

"How do you watch over another adult?" he asks me now, a year before his eightieth birthday. It's a question that has troubled him. We've seen Uncle Tommy twice in twenty-seven years, a separation that has never been explained to my satisfaction. In the late 1960s he simply faded from our lives. At times he and his wife Sandy have lived within miles of us—his six children, my cousins, raised as strangers. This is Dad's great regret: allowing two brothers, Herb and Tommy, to drift from the family.

Since boyhood I have heard my uncles, aunts, and parents talk about Tommy as if he were a great, unsolvable mystery. At Christmas, Uncle Teddy would be rolling through one of his many tales—perhaps the one about his surprise circumcision—and after the story had ended, in the lull that followed the laughter, someone would mention Tommy and soon the whole group would be repeating the same theories about what had gone wrong. With Herb the lack of contact could be explained. He did, after all, live on another continent and he always had been something of a lone wolf. But with Tommy it made no sense. Maybe he was mad, maybe he was sick, maybe he had gotten entangled with the mob, been placed in a witness-protection program, and avoided contacting us out of concern for our safety. When they talked about it, there seemed no urgency in getting answers. Underlying the discussion was a belief that eventually he'd make contact. He had their phone numbers; they hadn't moved. Someday he would call.

Earlier this decade I sensed a change in how my father felt about this. Tommy's and Herb's absences grew large in the years after Uncle Teddy and Uncle Clem died; they grew larger yet after Mom passed away. Dad no longer assumed that someday the call would come.

Two years ago I checked the phone books for a Tom Stankiewicz and found one. It was my uncle's namesake, his son, my cousin, and the call led to a crowded family reunion at which Dad, Uncle Tom, Aunt Bernice, and their spouses and children and grandchildren gathered. It was a first step, but it offered no opportunity for Dad and Uncle Tom to connect privately. It was a reunion for an audience, for us of the following generations, and it provided few answers, no closure, no sense of permanence, no vanquishing of the void.

If we have felt loved as children, we yearn as adults to give back to our parents. We try to repay them with time and attention for all the gifts they bestowed never expecting any in return. We yearn to show them that their investment paid off and to prove that the sacrifices were worthwhile. We aim to make up for the sleepless nights we caused while out late with friends speeding through subdivisions and sipping Boone's Farm wine. We aim to erase the little injustices we did, the times we doubted them, the times we chastised them for something as silly as jangling the coins in their pockets.

I want so much to make Dad's family whole again, to relieve his regret.

"Dad, if I invited Uncle Herb and Uncle Tommy to a game, do you think they'd come?"

"I doubt it," he says.

Then he looks toward the ball field, wanting to change the subject. "Old Weaver's not very sharp today."

—— **Oakland 6 ◇ Detroit 2** ——

Jeff Weaver lacks control.

◇ ◇ ◇ ◇ ◇ ◇ ◇   *Chicken Legs*

Grandpa
Stankiewicz.

**Game 17: Wednesday, May 12** ◇ In the upper deck behind home plate, Al the Usher, Aloysius Kopytko, wipes a rail clean.

"Heck, I wouldn't come here if I didn't have to," he says. "It's cold."

I see Al every game. The fire escape at the back of the press box empties into his section. He enjoys reading the media packet and I always sneak him one. Al is seventy-seven. He started at the park twelve years ago when the team won a division title.

"I like the Tigers and I like the people," he says. "Once in a while you get an asshole."

A fan since childhood, Al proves his allegiance by listing the 1934 pitching staff like a teacher taking attendance. " 'Schoolboy' Rowe, Tommy Bridges, Fred Marberry, 'Chief' Hogsett, 'General' Crowder, Elden Auker . . ."

For this year anyway, he guards the best seats in baseball and he evicts anyone who dares sneak in without a ticket. Tonight the cold air and Al's vigilance will keep those seats empty.

Below on the field, Oakland's Tony Phillips taps Alan Trammell's shoulder. They played together in the early 1990s. Though cordial—I doubt he's capable of anything less—Trammell hasn't forgotten yesterday when Phillips, forty, tried to incite a brawl after rookie Jeff Weaver threw wild and pelted him on the rear.

Phillips and Trammell make small talk about staying in shape late in a career. Finally Phillips says what he came to say, spinning last night's events in his favor.

"[Weaver] shouldn't be doing that," he says, his voice high-pitched, almost whiny. "I told him I'm too old to fight."

During the game it occurs to me that the people—Howard Stone, Al the Usher, Art and Amzie and Harwell and Trammell—aren't all that have become familiar. There's a routine that accompanies every game: the ceremonial first pitch, the dance of the mascot, the birthday song, the animated tigers racing on the scoreboard, the taped version of "Take Me Out to the Ball Game." At some point I will tire of it and it will spiral into a nightmarish dream sequence, like one from a 1950s cult movie, with a kaleidoscope of images swirling to the freakish sounds of a calliope.

"You can get too much of a good thing," my mom used to say. As a boy I loved her peanut-butter cookies. After school one afternoon she baked a huge batch and left them on the counter to cool while she ran errands. I snuck one and then several and ended up devouring the whole plate. To this day peanut-butter cookies gag me.

I hope my baseball gluttony doesn't have the same effect. I love this sport, but will eighty-one games be too much?

—— **Oakland 2** ◇ **Detroit 1** ——

Tony Phillips's outstanding catch saves the victory after pitcher Justin Thompson beans him. Detroit manager Larry Parrish warns his players, "This ain't no beer-league softball game."

**Game 18: Friday, May 14** ◇ The former short-stop emerges from the dining room into the shadowy concourse and a fan in his fifties notices immediately.

"Hello, Eddie Brinkman," he says.

With his long neck and bald head, Brinkman, fifty-seven, resembles a turtle. He nods and smiles at the man.

A boy can have more than a single hero. For one season, Eddie Brinkman filled the role for me. To be devoted to Brinkman made you a sixth-grade oddity because he never looked like a ballplayer. When he batted he squatted at the plate like a thin cowboy too long on the horse. His batting average, .224 lifetime, could barely boil water. But Brinkman could play shortstop as well as anyone; he went seventy-two games once without committing an error, a record at the time.

" 'Steady Eddie' Brinkman," Ernie Harwell called him.

He was the kind of fielder I imagined myself to be. Sure-handed, dependable, not flashy. During his string of perfect games I played short for a St. Malachy team.

"I hit like Honus Wagner and field like Eddie Brinkman," I boasted to Uncle Teddy.

My uncle had no children and few encounters with an

eleven-year-old's inflated self-image. But he knew enough to smile as he gave my dad, his younger brother, a quizzical look.

"Is Tommy that good?"

"He's good, all right," Dad said in such a way that I believed him.

Brinkman, a scout with the Chicago White Sox, remembers his four seasons in Detroit as his best. He thinks of the division title in 1972, of his fielding records, and of the noise.

"When the fans come from all sides, it's deafening," he says. "It's almost impossible to hear. It's sad to see the old park go. It happened to Comiskey. It happens to them all."

—— **Cleveland 4** ◇ **Detroit 2** ——

Brian Moehler, returning after a ten-day suspension for doctoring a ball, pitches well against first-place Cleveland. Gabe Kapler's two-run homer isn't enough.

**Game 19: Saturday, May 15** ◇ Al the Usher isn't thinking about Alice Cooper, the rock star, who is here today. Al has something more bothersome gnawing at him: Cleveland fans.

"They're cocky and they don't tip and they try to sneak into these seats," he says.

The aisles brim with an occupying army of middle-aged men in red socks and Bob Feller jerseys. Jacobs Field sells out continuously, turning Cleveland supporters into nomads. Almost 20,000 have stormed our park today.

In the lower deck, the Manleys of Ohio settle into their seats, twenty feet behind support beams. One post falls to the left of home and the other near first base.

"I guarantee that whining isn't going to make that pole disappear," says Chris Manley to his sons Stephen, eleven, and Peter, fourteen. Then he turns to me. "This is definitely a cool stadium."

The boys bought tickets as a Christmas gift for their parents. The youngest feels cheated.

"I can't see the scoreboard and I can't see first," he says.

By one estimate three of four seats have obstructed views. It's because of the steel posts that support the upper deck. In the newer, cantilever-type parks the top seats are farther from the field, so there are no beams in the way.

From their spot behind home the Manleys can see Alice Cooper fine.

His usual black wardrobe brightened by a Tiger jersey, the fifty-one-year-old entertainer tosses out the day's third ceremonial first pitch. Cooper, whose rock albums carry titles like *Killer* and *Alice Cooper Goes to Hell*, follows the representative of a Christian organization that drew 5,000 to an early-morning ballpark service. The son of a preacher, Cooper grew up in the blue-collar suburbs. Long before he took the name of a sixteenth-century witch, he was Vince Furnier, a kid who spent summers playing ball.

"If somebody had told me that you have a choice of being a big rock star or playing left field for the Tigers, there would not have been a choice at all," he says. "I would have said, 'Where's my locker?' "

Cooper went to his first game in the 1950s.

"We weren't rich or anything but my dad got tickets for a doubleheader. It was the Tigers against the Indians. I had never been to a big-league stadium in my life. All I knew of baseball was that you went out and played. At the park you're walking up the ramp and all of sudden it's all grass and it's green. There was the sound of batting practice, guys hitting the ball, that nice hollow sound in the stadium. The crack of the bat. To this day I can remember the thrill of that. I was just standing there in awe, going, 'This is heaven.' I was seven and baseball meant everything to me.

"I don't think I flinched," he says. "I got in one position and I just sat there with my mouth open for eighteen innings. I remember everything about it. I remember what the hot dogs tasted like. I remember the Cokes. If I had sat there for eight hours and nobody had bought me a Coke, it wouldn't have mattered."

When his son turned seven, Cooper broke from a concert tour and brought him to the park.

"We went in and he said, 'Wow, look at this.' I got to relive the whole thing. It was the Tigers against the Indians, by coincidence, and it was just great. Cecil Fielder hit a grand slam and there was a bench-emptying brawl in the second inning. It was everything you ever wanted in a baseball game."

At the peak of his fame in the mid-1970s, Alice Cooper was idolized by a million kids. His own hero, meanwhile, wasn't a musician.

"Let me tell you," he says. "I've met Sinatra. I've met the Beatles, the Rolling Stones, Dylan, Groucho Marx. Everybody you can imagine, I've met. The only time I ever got tongue-tied was with Al Kaline. I'm playing golf and I'm getting ready to hit the ball. I'm pretty composed most of the time. I'm a four handicap. I look back and there's a foursome behind me. And there's Al Kaline. I was literally speechless."

Alice and I, it seems, have something in common.

—— Cleveland 12 ◇ Detroit 7 ——

Five straight losses and the Tigers' big hitters, Bobby Higginson and Tony Clark, are struggling.

**Game 20: Sunday, May 16** ◇ Richie Rau—
"Chicken Legs" to his football friends from high school—works
in the narrow confines behind the center-field scoreboard. It's
a *Phantom of the Opera* sort of place—dark and dreary,
stuffy, sometimes unbearably hot, unseen by most, and inac-
cessible to all but a few—with two levels roamed and ruled by
one lone figure, a bone-thin man who wears jeans and T-shirts
and a faded Zig-Zag tattoo.

There is no elevator. To get here Rau walks through the
bleachers up to the top bench, occasionally stepping around a
drunk ("Drunks are easier than kids; you can move them out
of the way"), to a fenced-in staircase with a gate he chain-
locks behind himself. If there were a fire and his keys were
misplaced, he'd be trapped.

A journeyman technician, Rau has many responsibilities,
but none greater than maintaining the scoreboard. It's operated electronically now by someone in a booth on the opposite end of the park, someone who helps create what they call
"stadium atmosphere." Rau's role is to ensure that the Sony
Jumbotron screen and the less-sophisticated matrix message
board work.

When Navin Field opened, games weren't broadcast on
radio and there wasn't a public-address system. Ushers
announced lineups through megaphones. Though this park
wasn't built with electronics in mind, a system was patched
together in the decades that followed, and completely redone
in the late 1970s when the quaint, hand-operated scoreboard
was replaced.

"Guys have been doing their own shortcuts for years," says
Rau. "I had to figure it out because they didn't write any of it
down. I spent three years tracking it. I fixed it good. We keep
it going by junk."

In his bulb-lit area, paint peels from gray beams and the air
hangs heavy. Huge fans, like airplane props, allegedly draw

the heat outside. "I had to scrape a bird off of that," he says, looking at a blade.

Rau has a closet-size office with a workbench, an air conditioner, a monitor that shows what's on the scoreboard, and a radio that has spotty reception because of the power being kicked out by the mammoth screen.

It's relatively clean up here. Behind the ad billboards that flank the scoreboard, however, two dead pigeons lie in dirt and rust. But they don't bother anyone. "I'm going to have to get rid of them," he says. "They started roosting in here over winter. There was pigeon shit six inches deep. I had pigeon shit everywhere."

As a sports fan, he gets frustrated because he doesn't see the game while it's being played. Up in his perch he can't watch the action. He can peek through a straw-size hole in an ad banner, but it's no way to take in a game. So while he's working at the ballpark he has a VCR at home taping the contest, and if the Tigers win he watches when he gets there.

Rau learned his trade in the Marine Corps and he makes it clear that he is good at what he does. My knowledge of electronics ends at the light switch but I believe him. He exudes a confidence that extends beyond his trade skills. "If I would have chosen baseball instead," he says, "I would have been a professional baseball player."

Rau starts telling me about resistors and amp clusters and soon I'm smiling and nodding as if I know the difference. All the while I'm peeking down at the people beneath the scoreboard and imagining it is sixty years ago and that my grandpa is there, in his favorite spot, smoking a Swift Knight cigar and bragging about Barney McCosky, a hard-hitting rookie—and Polish, too. All of his favorite players were short or Polish; in other words, made in his own image.

For Grandpa the summit of the bleachers was the choice place to watch a game. The scoreboard shades you from the sun, the field is laid out before you, and you can see the plays unfold. The view provides a baseball panorama. By 1939 most of his children were adults. Herb would have been twelve; Tommy, five. I wonder if he ever sat on that bench and dreamt what their lives would be like, whether he ever imagined his sons would drift apart, like ice on the river.

I wonder that about my own sons. I picture them being close long after I'm gone. But you don't really know. It was probably what my grandpa wanted for his boys, too.

Rau draws my attention to something called an H-board but I'm not much interested and he notices.

"If they wanted to keep the stadium, all they would have to do is paint it and change the wiring," he says. "Just cause you're getting something new doesn't mean it's better."

—— **Detroit 9** ◇ **Cleveland 3** ——

Jeff Weaver ends the losing streak. Bobby Higginson hits two home runs and knocks in five. Tony Clark records his one-hundredth career homer.

◇ ◇ ◇ ◇ ◇ ◇   *A Place in the Shade*

**Game 21: Monday, May 24** ◇ Beneath a bruised sky Heather Nabozny darts onto the diamond, her walk so determined that it bends her forward at the waist. Her ground crew grips the edge of a tarp, fighting off a wind that has slipped under it and swelled it like a parachute. Fans cheer as they struggle to uncover the field. It is the kind of evening—a cold one, temperature in the 40s—where folks drape themselves in blankets, point to the 125-foot flagpole swaying in center, and wish away the rain clouds. Stripped of its canvas, the damp clay infield has lost its reddish hue. It is brownish gray with a hint of purple when pitcher Brian Moehler scratches his father's initials onto the mound.

In the upper deck beneath the first-base stands, Mary Pletta grills hot dogs, turning them with a fork. Tonight she's selling more coffee and hot chocolate than beer. From afar, her concession stand, number 34, looks like a lonely scene from an Edward Hopper painting, the light from behind the counter dusting the dark concourse with melancholy.

Mary and I have much in common. Her daughter lives in New Baltimore, the same small town where I live, and her grandchildren go to school with my boys. One plays baseball with William and Taylor, and another belongs to the National Junior Honor Society with Zack. Tomorrow I am scheduled to be here, missing Zack's induction ceremony and yet another of the twins' games—William might pitch this one.

Six weeks ago, at the dawn of this adventure, I knew the Tigers' schedule would clash with my family's. The decision was easy then. Now it tugs at my conscience and I'm unsure what to do. A decent father would skip the Tiger game.

—— **Toronto 12 ◇ Detroit 6** ——

The Blue Jays score ten runs in the seventh inning off Brian Moehler, Matt Anderson, and Will Brunson.

**Game 22: Tuesday, May 25 ◇** This morning Beth convinced me to go to the park.

"I'll tape Zack's ceremony," she said, "and you can see William and Taylor play next week."

The boys didn't object either, or if they did, they objected in silence.

At the game I seek out John Lee Davids. I need to talk to someone who won't lament the loss of this field in one breath and in the next acknowledge the need to replace it. I had heard about John and his battle to save Tiger Stadium. To understand it, you need to go back twenty years to when he and Judy were dating.

"Tiger Stadium was one of the few things we could afford," he says.

For two bucks apiece they could get into the bleachers. It was there they grew to be baseball fans, catching fifty to sixty games a year by the mid-1980s, always arriving early, chatting through the fence with the players as they warmed up in the outfield, eventually befriending several of them (Kirk Gibson, George Brett, and Jack Morris). Over time they discovered others with whom they shared the passion: writers, artists, musicians, and a Zamboni driver they called "Baseball John."

"After a while, baseball became secondary to seeing all our friends," he says.

In 1984 John Lee Davids's status at the park took a remarkable turn. While a graduate teaching assistant at the University of Michigan, he met team owner Tom Monaghan. That winter, John, an architecture student with a rockabilly pompadour, redesigned the owner's box for the pizza magnate. On opening day he and Judy were in the box with Al and Louise Kaline. By then they were living in one of Monaghan's Frank Lloyd Wright homes.

Three years later, after rumors surfaced of a new ballpark, the Tiger Stadium Fan Club was born. John and Judy lived in London at the time. John joined the fight in 1989 and developed the Cochrane Plan, an extensive proposal to renovate the facility and keep the team at Michigan and Trumbull. He thought his history with Monaghan would get the group face-to-face consideration; it didn't. The grassroots club grew to more than 11,000 members and for several years succeeded in blocking Monaghan. In 1992 Monaghan sold the team.

Tonight John, thirty-nine, sits in his favorite spot, the lower bleachers, with Willie Mays, his curly-headed three-year-old. Judy and their older boy, Dylan, are at a soccer game.

"I love the view from these seats," says John. "In the good seats you can see the hitter and pitcher. Here you can be right next to the action. Tiger Stadium is just a great building for baseball. It's an engineering marvel. The whole purpose was to put a lot of people close to the action. Baseball stadiums were not about pastry shops and crap like that. This stadium was built in Detroit, a workingman's town, for workingmen. The richest person and the poorest person sit next to each other. As an architect the greatest thing you can do is create a significant place for people. I don't think there's another place that means as much to the people of Michigan."

The bleacher crew John and Judy came to love has disintegrated.

"Since the stadium fight, we got so bitter we haven't really come to many games until this year," he says. "We have a hard time giving the team money. We got a look at the ugly side of baseball and how little baseball cares about common fans. I'm just coming this year because I want my kids to get some experiences here. Myself, I'm not interested in baseball anymore."

On that point John and I differ. I could never surrender baseball. I could boycott games toward a goal. I could stop listening on the radio, as I did when Harwell got fired. But I could never give up the game entirely because too much of my life has revolved around it. I wonder if John wouldn't love to be able to love the game again.

"It really makes me mad that our priorities are so screwed up that greedy baseball owners can get $200 million out of the public coffers," he says. "Every study shows that if you're going to invest a couple hundred million, a stadium is a terrible waste. Stadiums create seasonal jobs. I think once the stadium is done, Mike Ilitch will sell the team for a huge profit."

John can argue the issues persuasively but it really doesn't matter anymore. He is here for his sons. "I want the boys to remember it," he says.

On this Tuesday, Willie is more intrigued by the cotton candy. John doesn't say what I suspect he knows: Willie Mays won't remember this place and Dylan, six, may not. It will be up to their father to tell them about it.

—— **Toronto 5 ◇ Detroit 3** ——

The Tigers lose their third straight.

**Game 23: Wednesday, May 26 ◇** During batting practice, Bill Eisner, the former team photographer, gives me a picture he took. It shows me on the field, off to the side, taking notes.

"I caught this guy spying on the Tigers," he says.

Sometimes it feels that way, especially leaning against the batting cage, where I work at being inconspicuous by feigning interest in the nuances of the batters' swings, by following their hits with scrunched brows and analytical eyes, all the time listening to players and coaches and searching for a sense of what they're like and what they talk about among their own. And, too, I am acting oblivious to the fact that Lance Parrish is to my left and Alan Trammell to my right. They joined the Tigers at the start of my senior year in high school in 1977. They are coaches now.

I am sixteen years older than a few of these ballplayers. I know better than to idolize them. Still, I can't help feel that by having made it to the big leagues they are apart from the rest of us and that by being here on their field by their batting cage, I am out of place, a spy in the sun.

At game time I find the perfect antidote—in the shaded lower bleachers in right-center, a place for fans, where yesterday I met John Lee Davids. In the absence of TV monitors, Ernie Harwell's voice comes over cone-shaped speakers which in their tinniness allow you to imagine yourself fifty years back in time. There is an ethereal glow on this late afternoon, with the sun over left field silhouetting the cottonwood seedlings that float on the breeze. Gabe Kapler is in center, looking like he walked out of *Field of Dreams*, his pant legs high, contrary to team fashion, and his sculpted calves covered by the blue of his stirrups, a style that recalls the days of Ty Cobb, the days of my grandfather. I've been thinking a lot about Theodore Stankiewicz and his sons, scattered about this planet as they are, some separated geographically, others emotionally.

In times of great closeness—during those early days on Montlieu Street—who would have envisioned the separation? When day-to-day life flourished with activity—with new relationships, with children, with careers and interests—who would have thought twice about the distance?

At the time of my birth in 1960, all of the Stankiewicz children, except for Tommy, had married and settled into their own lives. Clem, an executive on the other side of the state, and Bucky, a photographer and sculptor in California, had dropped the family name, as Dad would do later. Clem became a Stone, pilfered from Jonathon Stone, a Tiger in the 1920s; Bucky became a Stanton. Ted, Irene, Dad, Bernice, and Tommy stayed in and around Detroit. Herb was in Asia. All kept in touch and Herb occasionally made his way back.

Twenty years on, Irene had passed, Herb rarely wrote, and Tommy had disappeared. "Why don't you try to track him down?" Mom asked Dad in private.

It's been almost another twenty years and five of Theodore and Anna Stankiewicz's children remain. Dad sees his sister Bernice regularly. She and her husband Ed celebrated their fiftieth anniversary and the room was filled with old friends, including the women who had stood up at her wedding, women who grew up on Montlieu Street. I knew from Aunt Bernice's twinkling smile that in her mind's eye it was just yesterday that her friends had been giggling and wondering about her brother Joey, the one with the wavy dark hair.

In the summer of 1996, Dad and I went to San Francisco to visit Bucky. The two of them talked for three days straight. Bucky recalled his knife-throwing exhibitions in the basement on Montlieu. "Phew, we were lucky," he said. They remembered Pa and Ma. They wondered about Herb and Tommy. They mourned Teddy and Clem. As our flight home left Uncle Bucky's California coast, I realized it might be the last time they would be together. My eyes were wet and Dad noticed. *Mr. Holland's Opus* was starting on the monitor.

"It's a sad movie," I explained.

Before coming to the ballpark today I called my friend from Milwaukee, Mike Varney. He's a lieutenant colonel in the Air Force, the same branch from which Uncle Herb retired. I asked Mike to help locate him.

Uncle Herb.

Out here far from home plate, even with the Tigers losing a fourth straight time, it feels mystic, as if anything is possible.

—— **Toronto 9** ◇ **Detroit 5** ——

Bobby Higginson and Gabe Kapler knock in two runs apiece.

**Game 24: Thursday, May 27** ◇ "Did you know that Metro Airport was rated the worst by CBS?" asks Zack.

This tidbit is one of a million facts in my thirteen-year-old's head. It has nothing to do with the ball game, which rookie pitcher Jeff Weaver has begun by retiring the White Sox in order.

"Doesn't surprise me," I say of the airport.

It's the two of us tonight and he's in a playful mood, plying our dialogue with one-liners.

When the scoreboard announces that this evening's Fan of the Game is from Kenosha, Wisconsin, Zack quotes John

Candy's polka-playing character in the movie *Home Alone*: " 'Kenosha. You know, home of the Kenosha Kickers.' "

When Gabe Kapler comes to the plate, Zack pushes his socks to his ankles.

"What are you doing?"

"Gabe Kapler has his socks up. I have mine down."

When the mascot, Paws, walks by in a uniform numbered 99—because this is 1999—Zack wonders, "What will the Tigers do in 2002?"

"What do you mean?"

"Well, Paws can't wear number 2, because it's been retired."

And soon: "Who played for the Detroit Lions and the Detroit Tigers?"

I can't think of a two-sport athlete.

"The organist," he says, and that moves the subject to music. He's still not talking about band camp and my lack of an invitation to chaperon. He hopes I will forget.

"Mr. Kleckner knows a lot about baseball. He's played the National Anthem at Tiger Stadium twice," Zack says. Kleckner is his band teacher and, as my son has reminded me numerous times, a member of Mensa.

I smile. Not because I've played the National Anthem; I haven't. Nor because I qualify for Mensa; I don't. I smile because if it came down to it, I could strike out Mr. Kleckner.

—— **Detroit 10 ◇ Chicago 5** ——

Jeff Weaver halts another losing streak. Luis Polonia, the newest Tiger—and at thirty-four, the oldest—gets five hits. He's made it back to the majors after two seasons in the Mexican League.

**Game 25: Friday, May 28** ◇ Backup outfielder Karim Garcia, the bambino of batting practice, pounds three balls off the facing of the third deck before the game. A fourth hits the light tower in right-center. Tonight he's wearing his uniform with socks on display, like Gabe Kapler. Anything to change his bad luck.

Ballplayers are a superstitious bunch.

Catcher Brad Ausmus, who earlier this week criticized his team's effort, did not shave today. The team won yesterday. Why risk it? When the Tigers swept the Yankees in April, manager Larry Parrish wore the same unwashed shirt for three days and Bobby Higginson crawled around the dugout for his lucky, 99-cent thumbguard, which the batboy had tossed by accident.

Who's to say it doesn't work?

In the fourth inning Garcia shoots a home run over the roof in right, marking only the thirty-fourth time it's been done. Ted Williams did it first, after the second deck was added in the late 1930s. Mantle did it three times; Norm Cash, four.

I'm in the concourse when Garcia's up and I miss his blast.

—— **Chicago 9** ◇ **Detroit 1** ——

**Game 26: Saturday, May 29** ◇ Allan Paschke makes it back to Michigan now and again and usually he winds up at the ballpark where he gets to thinking about many things: Norm Cash, the '61 season, and his dad.

"Detroit has changed a lot since my childhood but Tiger Stadium has been one constant here," he says. "It's one of the most beautiful places in the world."

He started coming when he was six with his father Lyle, a

high-school dropout who worked as a janitor and rose to a union presidency. "Baseball really brought us together," he says.

As a boy Allan liked first base—and Gail Harris, the guy who played it for Detroit in 1958 and 1959 before the Tigers obtained another.

"I remember the day," he says. "I was playing baseball in the backyard with Larry, my friend, and my dad broke the news that we had traded Steve Demeter for Norm Cash. I knew that Cash meant the end for Harris."

Harris, twenty-eight, batted five times in 1960. He got no hits and was sent west in May, never to play in the majors again. "I needed a new favorite player. Everyone wanted Kaline," says Paschke. "Norm Cash was the guy for me. It's hard to give a reason. I hooked up with him right away."

The attachment has lasted into adulthood. Paschke may have the world's most extensive Norm Cash collection. He has Cash jerseys, bats, photos, autographs, all of his ball cards, player contracts (he made $37,500 in 1969), a road uniform, one of Cash's belt buckles with the initials NC, even some of his traffic tickets. While in town for four games, taking a few days off from his job as a power-company executive in Vancouver, Washington, Paschke visited the cemetery where Cash is buried. Many of his baseball memories revolve around Stormin' Norman's best season.

"Sixty-one," he says. "I was eleven and twelve. It's the summer I remember best."

Bobby Lewis's "Tossin' and Turnin' " topped the charts; JFK was months into his first year in office; and everybody was watching *Gunsmoke* or *Wagon Train*.

"At Montgomery Ward, they had this Wilson Norman Cash baseball glove. I had been eyeing it for the longest time," he says. "I got it for my birthday. I still have it."

His words slide into a short silence. "This place evokes these kinds of memories for me."

Cash batted .361 that season to lead the league, and he hit forty-one home runs, four shy of Rocky Colavito, who had been traded to Detroit for Harvey Kuenn.

It would be impossible for Paschke to come here and not think about his father, who grew up near the park and cherished baseball, passing the love to his son. In 1966 at age forty-three, Lyle Paschke suffered his second heart attack, a fatal one. Allan was sixteen. By then they had made some great memories.

"When you're a kid," he says, "you think Harvey Kuenn is always going to play with the Tigers, Al Kaline is always going to be in right field, and your dad is going to live forever."

—— **Chicago 7 ◇ Detroit 1** ——

The Tigers have given up twenty-one runs in their last three games.

**Game 27: Sunday, May 30 ◇** From the roof of the stadium, the muffled cheers of the fans below sound ethereal, carried toward the heavens on a light breeze. There may be no better spot in this ballpark than way up here in what they call the "press overflow" area. It's as high as you can get without scaling the light towers or walking atop the place and there's no window to shield you from the elements. It is open to the air.

From this point above third base, you can see beyond the ballpark. Albert Kahn's Fisher Building, a golden-spired treasure, pierces the horizon on the left. The classic Book Tower, with its Italian Renaissance sculptures, stands thirty-seven stories high, over foul territory to the right. In center, bolting from the landscape beyond the scoreboard, are the limestone walls of the Masonic Temple near Cass Tech High School, where my dad went. All were standing in 1935, in what might have been the biggest year in Detroit baseball history.

Dad was fifteen and among the seventy-four eighth-graders under the charge of Sister Mary Grace Alexis, who had been persuaded to allow her class to listen to Ty Tyson broadcast the World Series on a radio one boy had brought from home. It was a Monday—October 7, 1935—and the Detroit team was up three games to two over Chicago. The Tigers had been to the Series a year earlier against Ducky Medwick, Dizzy and Daffy Dean, and the St. Louis Cardinals' Gas House Gang. This time, again, they were one victory from the championship.

Holy Name School stood along Nuernberg behind Holy Name Church, three-quarters of a mile from Montlieu Street. It was a rectangular building of brown brick with three levels and tall arched windows. The school had no gymnasium, and children who didn't go home for lunch ate at their desks. Most days Dad had ring bologna with ketchup on day-old pumpernickel.

Sister Alexis's room featured a U.S. flag, framed pictures of Presidents Washington and Lincoln, and a statue of the crucifixion. Gentler than some of her Dominican sisters, she was secretly called Sister Ex-Lax by the boys. But on this afternoon, with the game on the radio, they weren't thinking about that or long division or even the mountainous bosom of their classmate Yvonne.

They focused instead on Tommy Bridges's every pitch and hoped, as the game entered the ninth inning and the end of the school day neared, that Flea Clifton, Mickey Cochrane, or Charlie Gehringer would break the tie. Cochrane, the manager, singled and moved to second on a Gehringer grounder. With two outs, Goose Goslin, nicknamed for the way he flapped his arms when he ran, brought Cochrane home.

The room erupted in cheers just before the three-thirty school bell clanged. The celebration poured out the doors onto the playground and into the streets. At Navin Field fans hung around for an hour chanting for Goose Goslin. On Montlieu that evening, kids pounded iron skillets with wooden spoons. Grandpa brought home-bottled root beer up from the pantry and even Tommy, twenty-one months old, got a sip. Grandpa praised the brilliance of Cochrane and the talent of little Tommy Bridges. The Tigers had won their first world championship and the city partied all night.

In 1935 these press boxes would have been decked in red, white, and blue bunting, and a news reporter seated up here would have looked out and seen some of the same buildings in the distance. What he wouldn't have seen is the tip of a crane a mile beyond right field, where a thousand workers are erecting Comerica Park.

—— **Detroit 3** ◇ **Chicago 2** ——

Dave Mlicki pitches seven shutout innings. Gabe Kapler scores twice.

◇ ◇ ◇ ◇ ◇ ◇ ◇   *Mr. McGwire*

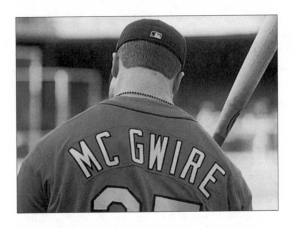

**Game 28: Friday, June 4** ◇ Two hours before game time, with the gates open early, crowds thicken around the visitors' dugout. This weekend Mark McGwire, the era's biggest baseball star, will bring an additional 60,000 to 70,000 people into the stadium where he hit his first home run. He likes it here. He is one of only four players to hit a ball over the left-field roof, a 514-foot shot. He has hit more road-game home runs at this park than anywhere else and there's great anticipation.

McGwire emerges from the clubhouse tunnel, his head lowered because the passageway wasn't made for men six foot four. Reporters huddle around him. The attention intensified last season as he pursued and broke Roger Maris's record. McGwire crossed the plate, lifted his son, and kissed him for the world to see. Today he is polite but weary of the questions.

Any chance you'll hit another one out of Tiger Stadium?

"I don't think about it."

Is it fun to play in this park?

"It's always fun to play this game."

Are you getting tired of interviews?

"People have got to get tired of hearing the same things all over."

What do you want to talk about?

"I don't want to talk with you guys."

What will you miss about this place?

"Everything," he says, a little warmth seeping into his voice. "This is it. It's baseball."

From the stands a man yells at the reporters, "Get out of the way so we can see him."

Afterward McGwire joins his teammates, bending and stretching on the grass. Photographers point telescope-sized lenses at him, snapping when he turns their way. Fans with banners and jerseys and Cardinal caps and huge portraits call out to him. A little girl pleads in a Shirley Temple voice, "Mr. McGwire. Mr. McGwire."

Across the field, catcher-turned-coach Lance Parrish signs balls for a few kids.

"I thought you guys came here for Mr. McGwire," he teases.

A commotion arises when McGwire, his eyes shaded by dark, face-hugging glasses, makes his autograph appearance. He works his way from the dugout to the netting behind home, accompanied by a police officer. He stands back three feet, signing selectively—there is no other way. He chooses courteous kids with lit eyes and stunned smiles.

"Mr. McGwire, Mr. McGwire. Thank you, Mr. McGwire."

Photographers document every step, some shooting from below to give him Pattonlike stature, others focusing on the outstretched arms that reach toward him like Adam to God in Michelangelo's masterpiece.

Rich "Chicken Legs" Rau, prepping the mike for the National Anthem, darts out of the way as the entourage approaches. Suddenly McGwire breaks for the batting cage. A cheer rises when he steps to the plate—genuine, unsolicited applause. He rewards it by pounding balls into the upper deck in left. One bangs the roof and rolls into the street. Another exits the park near the foul pole. Even the opposing Tigers are on their dugout steps watching: Higginson, Trammell, Moehler, Kapler.

This must be what it was like when Babe Ruth came here and my uncles Clem and Bucky, just boys, cheered his mammoth swings at Navin Field. There was no upper deck in the outfield and Ruth would knock balls into the street. One in 1926 registered as Ruth's longest, 626 feet officially, much longer when Uncle Clem told of it. After his wife had been institutionalized my uncle would take a cross-state bus to Detroit and stay with us every Christmas. As a boy I cherished Uncle Clem's visits, for he'd regale me with stories of the Bambino and Ty Cobb and Harry Heilmann and Heinie Manush and "Fat Bob" Fothergill, who couldn't possibly have played had he been as big as my uncle described him. An admitted ham, Uncle Clem didn't feel confined by the facts, though I didn't know it then. In his stories Cobb had razor-sharp spikes, caked with dried blood, and Ruth devoured a dozen hot dogs between innings. Uncle Clem recalled his childhood in detail: the way bacon-grease sandwiches stuck to the roof of his mouth and how accusations of cheating rose from the kitchen when adults played cards over quart jars of home brew and how a neighborhood hockey game ended with a bloody slash across Father Leahy's face after the priest had delivered a hard check. To a child's ear the twenties and thirties sounded like a gritty adventure, a poverty endured with humor and ingenuity, and baseball was always part of it. In the retelling men like Ruth grew to mythic proportions and my uncles and father grew right along with him.

After the National Anthem, Mark McGwire traces a cross on his chest with his ball cap. On the mound, pitcher Brian Moehler draws the initials *FM* into the clay and proceeds to retire the first two hitters, which brings up McGwire. He gets a hero's welcome. But he flies to shallow right on the first pitch. In the fourth the park sparkles with camera flashes as McGwire swings. Some boo the Detroit first baseman for catching the ball. In the sixth, after two big misses, McGwire bounces to second. In the ninth he gets one final chance. With the crowd standing, he grounds to short, ending the game.

Maybe tomorrow.

—— **Detroit 4** ◇ **St. Louis 1** ——

Brian Moehler limits the Cardinals to four hits in seven innings.

**Game 29: Saturday, June 5** ◇ Near the batting cage, several Latin American players chat in Spanish and Bobby Higginson teases rookie Gabe Kapler. Higginson is in a good mood and soon he moves on to Mark McGwire, asking about his bat. Later he remarks to another player, "They're really flying today. McGwire might hit the scoreboard."

That would please Rich "Chicken Legs" Rau. He'd love for McGwire to send one off the Jumbotron screen, a nearly impossible feat. If it happened, Rau would present the broken lights to McGwire as a memento.

Yesterday, while reporters questioned the St. Louis star, I snapped photos. Today a sportscaster approaches me about them. At first, because of his evasive manner, I suspect he runs a memorabilia business on the side and wants to buy my prints. (Selling them would violate Tiger media policy and jeopardize my pass.) "I just want a picture of me with McGwire so my mom will know I have a real job," he confesses eventually. "He's the only ballplayer she's heard of."

In the stands, waving from the box seats, my brother catches my attention; he's with his son Shawn. Though he turned forty-five this year, I still call him Joey and he still calls me Tommy. He motions with his camera and I know to hold my pose while he takes a few shots of me on the field by the cage with players in the background. The first time I came to the park was with my brother. It was a school night, a Thursday in September 1968. Some fans recall everything about their first game, from the score to the big hits. I recall little, and if history hadn't embossed that night I might know nothing of it. Not yet a baseball fan, I was oblivious to the fact that Detroit had earlier clinched the American League pennant and that Denny McLain had already won thirty games. I was oblivious to almost everything about the game except that I, a seven-year-old, was with the older guys, Dad, Joey, and two of Joey's pals, and that we were out late. What I do remember are fragments: shivers in the cold, a tongue burnt by too-hot chocolate, a urinal that looked like a bathtub, and standing and cheering wildly, lost among the taller torsos, a sapling in the forest. We were cheering, I learned later, for Mickey Mantle, who hit a home run in his last appearance at the ballpark. McLain had served the ball as a gift.

It was Joey who taught me to step into the pitch like Kaline and to wait until Dad went to work before taping a strike zone on the garage door for rubber-ball target practice. By the time he got to high school Joey was the epitome of cool. He had been a halfback on the junior-high football team before deciding sports wasn't where it's at. He had black-light posters, a stash of *Playboy* magazines, and a red Midget that sometimes ran. He was vice president of his class and had a girlfriend that he would marry someday. Though separated by six years, my brother and I remain close—my sisters Jan and Colleen, too. I can't imagine living ten time zones away, seeing each other once in thirty-five years and not calling or writing in a decade. But that pretty much describes my dad's relationship with his brother Herb and that's on my mind today because my Air Force friend, Mike Varney, drove in from Milwaukee this morning by way of South Bend, Indiana, where he stood on the 50-yard line of the Notre Dame football field.

He has had no luck tracing Uncle Herb.

"It'll take some time," he says, ever the optimist.

I have my doubts that we will find Herb but I feel certain I will be able to reach my other distant uncle, Tom. I just don't know whether he will come if invited.

Zack is with Mike and me today.

"What kind of seats will they have at Comerica Park?" Zack wonders.

"They'll be wider, with more leg room."

"I hope they're leather recliners," he says.

There is no room to spread out today because Mark Mc-Gwire has packed the park again. Zack sits in the seat to my left, no space between us.

"Do you know how many lights are on those towers?" he asks, motioning at the roof.

I scrunch my shoulders and smile at him.

"You're a good kid, you know?"

"Ninety-six," he says. "Ninety-six lights."

—— **St. Louis 7** ◇ **Detroit 2** ——

Five Tiger pitchers give up runs.

**Game 30: Sunday, June 6** ◇ Al the Usher missed a few games earlier in the week.

"I had a mini-stroke," he says. "I'm fine now."

It's in the 90s and Al hopes for a quick game. The crowds are getting to him.

"They ask the same dumb questions over and over. 'When's Mark McGwire taking batting practice?' Not today. 'Did I miss Mark McGwire taking batting practice?' He's not taking it. McGwire's getting tired of it, too, and I don't blame him. . . . Hey, when are you going to bring your dad to a game?"

In the air-conditioned press box, sports columnist Joe Falls, eyes guarded by bulky sunglasses, blusters at a young radio personality.

"No wonder you failed in school," he says. "You don't listen. You don't listen to the teacher." Falls's teasing makes clear that he is the teacher.

A visiting reporter hearing Falls's loud voice remarks to no one in particular, "It's good to know some things never change."

—— **St. Louis 8** ◇ **Detroit 4** ——

The Tigers blow two leads. Shortstop Deivi Cruz hits a 400-foot homer, his first of the year. Mark McGwire gets none in the three-game series.

**Game 31: Monday, June 7** ◇ Long before Bill
Eisner started shooting photos for the ball club, he promised
to marry his girlfriend, Sammie, if she could get tickets to the
1968 World Series. She came through and they wed fifteen
months later. Bill, sixty-two, is at almost every game in a semi-
official capacity, a volunteer who takes on-field pictures. He
has had press credentials since 1976, the season of Mark
Fidrych. The Tigers have other team photographers now but
Bill continues to shoot, mainly for himself, frequently giving
photos to players and workers.

He introduced himself the second game of the season.

"A lot of these guys I talk to and get to know," he says outside the dugout. "They're here to play. I just like to take pictures. I don't make any money off it. It's a hobby."

He snaps thousands of shots a year and prints all of them.

"You never know when you're going to get a shot no one
else got," he says. One of them came in February 1993. Bill
also shoots for the city fire department and he was the lone
photographer at a tragedy that claimed seven children. His
picture of a firefighter with a dead child in arms played big on
page one and went international on the AP and Reuters wires.
A Detroit paper nominated it for a Pulitzer.

Bill notices Ernie Harwell walking our way.

"Ernie used one of my photos in a book," he says, timing
his words so Harwell hears.

"Bill takes fine pictures, wonderful pictures," Ernie replies.

Eisner puts Harwell on the spot.

"You two should get a picture together," he suggests.

"Maybe one of these days," I say.

"How about now?" Harwell asks.

We pose for two shots, arms around each other. Harwell
grins big beneath a red-starred cap that commemorates a
Negro League team. He looks as casual and comfortable as

usual: a button-up short-sleeve shirt and beige pants. His back feels bony and fragile, like my dad's.

Later I ask Bill what he plans to do with his collection of photos. "Do your children like baseball?"

"Well, my daughter could never walk or talk," he begins. I learn that she lives in a group home in another state, near Bill's wife, who has been in a nursing home since suffering a debilitating stroke. "I couldn't take care of them."

Bill has been coming to more games in recent years.

"I could be going to the bar and drinking," he says, aiming for levity.

—— **Detroit 9 ◊ Pittsburgh 4** ——

A wild Jeff Weaver lasts five innings. Damion Easley leads the attack with a single, double, and home run, knocking in three runs and scoring two. Will Brunson gets his first major-league win.

**Game 32: Tuesday, June 8 ◊ "Are you Baseball John?"**

Pedro Munoz looks at me, baffled by the question.

"I'm looking for a guy they call Baseball John."

"Nope, I'm Pete," he says.

I sit down anyway and Pete tells me about a game last year when Ken Griffey Jr. leaped high in center field and stole a home run from Luis Gonzalez. Pete was standing at the outfield fence in the lower bleachers, right there, by Griffey's glove, as shutters clicked and tape rolled. The catch made the TV highlights and *Sports Illustrated*, as did Pete.

Next week, when Griffey and the Mariners come to town,

Pete will bring a copy of the magazine that a friend pilfered from a doctor's office. "I want Griffey's autograph," he says.

Pete shows me his Cal Ripken glove, which has several unrecognizable signatures. "This guy's from Cincinnati," he says, tapping one. Next to it, I notice the large looping letters of Paws, the team mascot.

"I gave Paws an angel," he says. Pete has a dozen angels pinned to his Pirates cap.

For thirty seasons he's been coming to games, mostly alone in recent years. He has ten nephews and he used to invite the five who live in Detroit. They aren't interested anymore.

We sit on a blue metal bench, shaded from the sun, watching seagulls swoop and strut for control of a hot-dog bun in right field, and we talk about our favorite players, Kaline, Cash, Horton, Brinkman, Lolich.

"Aurelio Rodriguez," he says, recalling the Mexican-born third baseman who spent the 1970s in Detroit. "People used to ask me if I was his cousin. I'd say, 'No, he's my daddy.' "

He laughs. There is no relationship but some resemblance. Pete, thirty-nine, has curly black hair, sideburns that creep down his cheeks, and a crooked-tooth smile that comes easily to his round face. He has a memory for dates and scores and statistics—"Champ Summers hit twenty home runs that year"—and he knows a lot about the Tigers. I'm surprised when he says that soon he's going to buy his ticket for the final game.

Doesn't he know it sold out months ago?

—— **Detroit 11** ◇ **Pittsburgh 4** ——

Nelson Cruz records his first win in his first start. Juan Encarnacion gets four hits and scores three runs.

**Game 33: Wednesday, June 9** ◇ About the fourth inning, Al the Usher sneaks Dad and me into a pair of seats above Ernie Harwell's booth. We are closer to home plate than the shortstop.

It's been a hot day but now the sun hides behind the stadium, bathing the underbelly of the clouds in pink. On the field Pirates manager Gene Lamont argues strikes with the umpire. He props his hands on his hips and moves like a bobbing-head doll in the back of a '69 Camaro.

"Who's that remind you of?"

"Billy Martin," Dad says, recalling the abrasive manager who took the Tigers to the '72 playoffs. "They don't let them kick dirt anymore."

Martin gets us reminiscing and soon I bring up the batboy controversy, the great disappointment of my childhood.

It was 1975 and I was fourteen. I had flooded the Tigers with letters, begging to be hired as a batboy, promising to work for free. The team phoned once when a position opened. I was out playing and Mom took the call. We lived in the new suburbs and she hated the idea of me going to Detroit. I always suspected that she gently sabotaged my plans.

"You're too young," she said. "You have to be sixteen."

And if she had left it at that—simply stuck to the age requirement—I still would have been disappointed but not suspicious.

"Anyway," she continued, "how would you get down there every day? You can't drive and you're not taking the bus. It's dangerous. Things happen down there. Terrible things. People get murdered there every day."

You would think the fact that she had been through eight brain surgeries might grant her some immunity from the hormone-fueled anger of a young teen. Perhaps it would have after the initial surgery in 1969, when doctors first cut into her skull and removed a tumor. It was all so fresh then, the fears, the paralysis, the shaven head. But that had been six years earlier, and we had all grown accustomed—maybe even numb— to the almost-annual operations.

So I argued, and she argued back. My interrogation uncovered few details. Who called? What did he say? What did you say? Didn't you get his name? Is he going to call later? Don't he wanna talk to me? Can't I just work on Saturdays? Did you ask him?

"Well," she concluded, "it doesn't matter. You're too young. That's what he said."

Twenty-four years later I ask Dad, "Was that the real story?"

"Oh, yeah. Your mom didn't want you to do it but she knew you had your heart set. I told her I'd get off work early and take you. But you weren't old enough."

If it happened differently, Dad won't betray Mom with the truth. And there is no sense in asking him again. He'd only grow more adamant. He's stubborn that way. It took years to convince him to get a hearing aid. This talk of my age, though, gets him thinking.

"You know, I shouldn't have put you in school early," he says.

He wants my assurance for the minor fraud he committed thirty-some years ago, a crime that can be revealed now because the statute of limitations has long since expired.

"It worked out fine," I say.

But I wasn't so sure at age eleven when I found out. Dad was on his bed, sorting through a thin metal case that he stored on the top shelf in his closet. In it he kept important papers and savings bonds that never matured.

"Hey Tommy, here's your birth certificate," he said.

I studied it and then gasped. "They made a big mistake, Dad. It says December seventeenth."

He looked at me as if I were a question mark. "We told you, didn't we?"

He explained how in 1965 he and Mom hatched a plan to get me into school early. I was four at the time and the kindergarten cut-off date was December first. You had to turn five before then to enroll. Shortly after my sister Colleen was born in March, my parents apparently decided it would be easier on Mom, who was approaching forty-three, if I was out of the house a few hours a day. Whether this says more about her than me, I'm unsure.

Dad, a federal employee, worked in the photography department at a tank plant and he had access to darkroom equipment that allowed him to doctor pictures. (Once, he brought home an eight-by-ten glossy on which he had superimposed a third eye on his forehead.) So Dad altered my birth certificate, changing December to November, and registered me for school.

But the deceit did not stop there. They conspired to keep the silence, enlisting relatives and neighbors into the charade by holding elaborate sham birthday parties on November 17. I grew up thinking I was a Scorpio who would never get along with a Leo. After the truth surfaced, the false birthdays continued; I kept the secret, not wanting Dad to be hauled off to jail.

The early school start impacted me in one major area: sports. I developed late and my glaringly adequate talent didn't compensate for my small size. And that's why Dad is second-guessing himself. I never tried out for the high-school team and a year's growth would have made a difference.

Dad had the opportunity to play but didn't. As Dad's days at Holy Name School neared an end, Father Leahy paid a visit to Ma and Pa Stankiewicz. Dad had become known locally in football and baseball and the priest, accompanied by a prep coach, urged the Stankiewiczes to send their son to Catholic Central, a regional sports powerhouse. Father Leahy hinted that Notre Dame might eventually be interested in my dad's talents. As much as Pa wanted his boys to play professional sports, he knew the odds. He thought it more realistic for one of them to become an engineer. So Dad went to Cass Tech High School, where he promptly struggled with math. It was left to a later son, Tommy, to fulfill Pa's engineering dreams.

During my adolescence, Dad offered little career advice. Once he suggested I might become a firefighter because the job had a retirement plan. That was his main concern. "Get a job with a pension," he said. But that was it. He did show me Ty Cobb's unusual batting grip, his hands three inches apart, and he did demonstrate Uncle Bucky's much-heralded drag bunt method, though as a right-handed hitter I couldn't use it. And, baseball aside, there was the time he tried to convince me to carry my wallet in a front pocket—to deter the thieves who were hardly rampant on our smooth suburban sidewalks.

Most of the lessons we learn from our fathers come casually and naturally, not in grand speeches or insightful lectures or memorable demonstrations. We simply absorb their actions and behaviors and either embrace or reject them. From Dad I've learned that perseverance is more valuable than talent, that silence isn't the same as weakness, and that family is always family.

The last time we talked about a ballpark reunion with his brothers, he seemed reluctant. But I've been pursuing it anyway.

"Dad, I'm going to try to contact Uncle Herb and Uncle Tom."

"That's fine with me," he says, and we leave it at that.

—— **Pittsburgh 15** ◇ **Detroit 3** ——

Pirate Brant Brown clears the right-field roof.

◇ ◇ ◇ ◇ ◇ ◇ ◇ *Junior and Dutch*

Ken Griffey Jr.

**Game 34: Monday, June 14** ◇ Before the game Ken Griffey Jr. squeezes Gabe Kapler's muscular right calf as if measuring it.

"Hey, I got you there," he says, giving the rookie his gap-toothed grin.

Nearby, teammate Brian Hunter jokes that he has been helping Griffey with his hitting.

"Excuse me, Mr. Hunter," says Griffey. "Could you move your press conference over there?" He points to the upper deck.

It's all in humor. Still, no matter what skit is playing out, this is Griffey's show and he likes the spotlight.

In the batting cage Alex Rodriguez lines a ball to center.

"I got that," says Griffey, indicating he could have caught it.

Rodriguez rips another up the alley.

"Got that one, too," Griffey teases.

Bill Eisner, the photographer, edges toward me.

"The same sideshows go on every year," he says, arching his eyebrows.

Two months into this season, I have encountered three ballplayers destined for the Hall of Fame—Ripken, McGwire, and Griffey. A beacon of decency, Ripken struck me as a humble legend making his farewell tour. McGwire, a man of heroic proportions, had a presence that turned the heads of fellow major-leaguers. Griffey, probably the most talented, radiates a playfulness that draws others to him. Though he speaks an R-rated vocabulary, he looks boyish with his cap on backwards. At twenty-nine he is the youngest of the three and the only one not to make time for those seeking autographs.

Early in the game, Pete Munoz flaps his glove as Griffey, who took him onto the pages of *Sports Illustrated*, makes an over-the-shoulder, Willie Mays catch in deep center. Pete forgot his copy of the magazine. He vows to bring it tomorrow. He'd also like Griffey to sign a ball for a neighborhood waitress who recognized him from the photo.

In Pete's mind, the picture has joined him with Griffey in baseball history and he figures that will mean something to the Seattle star.

—— **Detroit 8 ◇ Seattle 7** ——

Down by five, the Tigers rally on two Gabe Kapler home runs and a ninth-inning Tony Clark double.

**Game 35: Tuesday, June 15** ◇ Elmore Leonard doesn't want to look foolish or feeble—who would? So he has prepared for this night when he will deliver the ceremonial first pitch. Over the weekend the seventy-three-year-old author loosened his left arm by throwing in his Bloomfield Village yard, which he hadn't done in years. The warm-up aimed to prevent the nightmare that haunts any self-respecting former player lucky enough to throw a ball on the field of his idols: the pitch in the dirt.

Little kids, elderly legends, and limp-armed neophytes can get away with it. Anyone else who bounces one to the plate lives with shame and regret. Leonard knows this.

I invited him to the park, figuring what the hell. I'm living out one fantasy—seeing all eighty-one games—I might as well pursue a few others. He surprised me by saying yes. The fringe benefits of this project extend well beyond free hot dogs in the press box. I love Leonard's books. I've skipped meals to continue turning the pages. There may be writers who are more literary—whatever that means—but I find no one more entertaining. Of course, I told him none of this.

A slender man with scratchy beard, Leonard talks in tranquil tones befitting his dry humor.

"I'm thinking of throwing a knuckleball," he says.

It's a pitch few professionals can control and it seems unlikely Leonard would attempt one. He does, however, enjoy surprises.

Leonard's family, all born in New Orleans, came to Detroit from Memphis, Tennessee, during the Depression and rooted the Tigers to their first world championship. The 1935 team featured Cochrane, Greenberg, Gehringer, and Goslin, as well as guys with nicknames like Schoolboy, Chief, and General; Jo-Jo and Gee; Flea, Firpo, and Freck.

Elmore got his own nickname at the Jesuit high school where he played first base. Teammates tagged him "Dutch," for the Washington Senators pitcher.

"What kid wants to be called Elmore?" he asks.

After thirty-five novels and more than a dozen films, he still answers to Dutch.

Leonard likes section 217 between home and third base above the cushioned chairs of the Tiger Den, where he could be sitting had he accepted team president John McHale's offer of better tickets.

"My folks sat here," he says. "This was the grandstands then, a buck-ten. This is where we always sat. In those days it was all green."

A few fans approach Leonard for autographs and the author obliges, struggling to write neatly on the curved surface of a baseball.

"I tried to get Marv Owen's and Goose Goslin's autographs out on Michigan Avenue," he says, recalling a 1930s encounter. "Owen pushed me aside."

Leonard notices that Seattle starter Frankie Rodriguez throws lots of curves and that reminds him of a right-hander who played parts of three decades with Detroit. "I remember watching Fred Hutchinson pitch and thinking they were going to kill him. It looked like he was lobbing it in, throwing nothing but junk. But he was hitting his spots."

Then there was Buck Newsom—"Bobo," he called himself and everyone else. He played twenty years, never lasting more than two straight seasons with one team. He led the Tigers to the 1940 pennant.

"My mother loved him. He was an undisciplined, raucous character. He looked like a beer drinker, a big beer drinker."

Leonard rates Ted Williams, Mantle, Gehrig, and Gehringer as the best players he saw. But his favorite was George

Kell, a third baseman from Swifton, Arkansas, who edged Williams out of the batting title by .0002 of a percentage point in 1949. Kell overtook Williams on the final day of the season and he was on deck in the ninth, with an opportunity to either increase his lead over Williams or lose it. But Eddie Lake ended the game on a double play. Leonard's admiration made its way into his 1969 novel *The Big Bounce*. Years later author and athlete met when Kell was a TV broadcaster.

"I told George Kell I would die happy if I could play catch with him," he says. "I'm fascinated by the arms these guys have, especially the third basemen. They throw so straight, hardly any arc on the ball. I can't imagine having that kind of arm. The ball just goes like that." He shoots out his left hand.

Between innings a woman in her forties raises a sign to coach Lance Parrish. *Happy Birthday, Lance*, it says. The guy behind her has a cap shaped like a beer mug. Does Leonard see his characters at the ballpark?

"You can't tell," he says. "That's the whole point about my characters. You can't tell what they do. You can't tell if they rob banks or roof houses."

Our conversation alternates between baseball and writing. His advice on the latter: Leave out the parts readers tend to skip.

Leonard got two contracts in the mail today for foreign rights. He has trouble imagining how they'll translate American ghetto slang into Czechoslovakian. "I think it's probably not going to be very good." His work appears in two dozen languages and his screenplays are in demand in Hollywood. John Travolta, Paul Newman, and Samuel L. Jackson have played his characters.

Most days Leonard writes from breakfast to dinner. This morning he was working on *Pagan Babies*.

"I never thought I'd hit the *New York Times* list," he says, nibbling on popcorn. "I didn't think I wrote well enough or poorly enough."

On the diamond a Seattle player slaps the ball into the hole between short and third. Deivi Cruz goes deep, snags it, stops, plants his right foot, and fires to first, beating the batter.

"Wow," says Leonard, not loud enough to merit an exclamation point. "God, isn't that amazing? It's a long throw. . . . I think this is the hardest sport to play. You're right out there in the open. Everybody's watching you. You've got to have the arm. You've got to know the game. It takes an awful lot of guts to stand up to a guy throwing ninety miles an hour. I can't believe these guys can actually see which way the ball's spinning."

After a cigarette break—by law fans can no longer smoke in their seats—Leonard watches the mascot Paws lead other people in the singing of "Take Me Out to the Ball Game."

"I feel sorry for him," he says.

I ask Leonard if he's going to miss Tiger Stadium—the park where he's been coming for sixty-four years with his parents, children, and grandchildren; the park where he has witnessed the legends of the sport, where he discovered George Kell— and he gives a quick answer.

"No," he says. On his face a grin simmers as if he's been waiting all night to deliver the punch line.

Leonard leaves before the game ends. He leaves with a souvenir jersey and an autographed ball and a bit of pride, for his ceremonial pitch floated over the plate without a bounce. And it gets no better than that.

Well, almost.

—— **Seattle 5** ◇ **Detroit 4** ——

**Game 36: Wednesday, June 16** ◇ Zack turned fourteen today and I'm at the park alone. It's a lousy place for a father to be on his son's birthday. Let's see: I've missed his Honor Society induction, his band concert, and now this. For what? An old ballpark? A team that plays pathetically?

This year we bought Zack some clothes, CDs, and Adlai Stevenson collectibles.

I have a hard time remembering the items my parents gave me, not to say I didn't appreciate them. I just can't recall the specifics. Undoubtedly there was the usual assortment of games like Yahtzee and Life and that electric football field with players who sometimes vibrated in the right direction. One year there was a used hardball signed by Red Schoendienst, with the inscription, *To my pal Greasy*, a character unknown to me. And that first baseball glove, a blue no-name model from K-mart—was that a gift? I was nine and can't remember.

"It don't move," I said, trying to flex it.

"You got to work it in," Dad explained. He took me into the garage to the bench beside the silver Bonneville convertible. He poured a few drops of car oil into the glove's palm and it spread like syrup. He massaged it in with his fingers. As the leather absorbed the oil, the glove took on a brown tint. He drizzled some more and let me try.

"Spread it all around," he said.

My fingers glided into the pocket and around the palm and up the edges.

"Do that every week and it'll get soft."

We played catch in the yard with a white tennis ball, he with his bare hands, me with my new glove.

Before bed we put Joey's black-taped ball into the pocket and tied the glove with twine so that its sides enveloped the ball.

Though we never believe it as children, the gifts we come to cherish most are rarely boxed or wrapped or bought. They are gifts of time.

Here at the ballpark, above me in section 212 by third base, catwalks connect the upper concourse to the top deck. Soon I feel a pelt on my right sleeve. Someone on the concourse missed the easy target, my balding head, and christened my shirt with a gob of spit.

Maybe I deserve it.

After the fourth inning I head home to be with Zack.

—— **Seattle 7** ◇ **Detroit 1** ——

The Tigers fall fifteen games behind first-place Cleveland.

**Game 37: Thursday, June 17** ◇ Manager Larry Parrish pulls Jeff Weaver before the ninth inning, this despite Weaver's one-run, five-hit performance. When the rookie reaches 105 pitches, his day is over. The Tigers are cautious with Weaver because they want to protect his young arm.

Ted Plaza, seventy-five, thinks it's silly.

"He should be able to blow his own game," says the former high-school coach. "I'm against the pitch count. When Mickey Lolich pitched, he pitched three hundred and some innings a year. There was no pitch count."

DeWayne Smith, sixty-three, tries to understand management's view. "Supposedly they're playing the statistics. But you've got to go by feeling a little bit. Ah, maybe that's why I'm not managing."

Smith and Plaza have seen hundreds of games together. In 1984, a world championship year, they went to at least thirty. By then they had already known each other for three decades. If you notice them at all, you probably notice two things. First, one's black and the other's white, and second, they wear ball caps that proclaim them Sports Sages in recognition of their proud affiliation with a Michigan-based coaches' group.

With Detroit up 2–1, C. J. Nitkowski starts the ninth inning.

"We used to say, 'You've got to get the leading lady,'" says Plaza. "There used to be a lot of slang in baseball."

Earlier in the night when Luis Polonia came up, Plaza proclaimed him "a slapper." When Higginson blooped one to center, he called it "a banana stalk." A double was "a deuce."

"Let's get the big man, the money man," says Smith, when Ken Griffey Jr. is announced.

In the dugout Jeff Weaver, his hair disheveled, palms his face and caps his hands over his mouth and nose as he watches each pitch with bulging eyes. The count goes to 3–2 on Griffey, who asked to start in center rather than as designated hitter in this, his last appearance at the park.

Griffey walks and Parrish brings in Todd Jones.

"Cross your toes and your fingers with this guy," says Plaza.

Jones falters, allowing a single and a triple, erasing Weaver's lead. The crowd boos.

Plaza picks up his orange-and-green pillow, which has a shag design on one side, and he and Smith head to the car before the game ends, as they always do.

After the loss Weaver, furious, leaves the locker room before reporters can talk to him; Jones, the veteran, stays and answers questions.

My mind is on tomorrow. Al Kaline will be at the park to broadcast. It might be the day.

—— **Seattle 4** ⬦ **Detroit 3** ——

Jeff Weaver gets a no-decision in a game he should have won.

◇ ◇ ◇ ◇ ◇ ◇ ◇  *Pa*

Grandpa
Stankiewicz
and Dad.

Dad bolted past the elms into the house on Montlieu. It was a Sunday afternoon in June 1957, a few years before my birth. Pa was sweating and pale and struggling to get his arthritic legs into a fresh pair of pants. He wanted to look his best; he always wanted to look his best. He grabbed his felt fedora as Dad and Uncle Tom rushed him through the French doors past the stained-glass window, with Grandma crying and praying and drawing a cross on his forehead.

"Damn it, Joe. My shirt."

They tucked his shirttail into his pants and sped off, Dad holding one hand on the horn and running red lights for five miles to Memorial Hospital. Pa grew incoherent and then silent in Uncle Tom's arms. He was breathing but unconscious when they arrived, too heavy to carry into the emergency room. Within the hour Theodore Stankiewicz had died.

In such times you think of many things.

Maybe Dad thought about the day forty years earlier when a baseball bat slipped from his hands and crashed through the side-door window. Before he could explain, Pa was walloping Teddy's behind and my dad was crying, "But I did it, I did it."

Pa stopped hitting Teddy.

"Spank him!" Teddy demanded, pointing at his younger brother. "You gotta spank him now."

"Well, I hit one of you," Pa said, exasperated, "I ain't gonna hit another."

Maybe Dad thought about how his father greeted every female, whether age three or eighty-three, how he would stop, stand straight, click his heels, and lift his hat, finishing with a slight tip of the head. If they were older Polish women, he would add the word "pani," a respectful title. In summer he carried scissors so he could snip rose stems and present them to passing "girlies."

Grandma would sometimes watch from the window. "Good old Teddy," she said, her voice touched with sarcasm. "Why doesn't he bring some of that sunshine into our house?"

Maybe Dad thought about how, while unemployed during the Depression, Pa would do odd jobs—give neighbors haircuts and sole their shoes—for free, or how in the alley behind the house he would pound dents out of his Chrysler supervisors' cars using tools he had made specially for the job.

Ma chided him for refusing their money.

"I'll have a big funeral someday," he said, chuckling.

Maybe Dad recalled the summer of 1952 and the one woman Pa couldn't win over, my mother's mother, Grandma Muse. The two of them, along with Grandpa Muse, a carpenter by trade, built my parents' first home. It was far from a peaceful project. Strong-willed Grandma Muse insisted on instructing Pa, a perfectionist in his own right, on the correct way to pour a footing, build a wall, and shingle a roof. Try though he did with compliments, laughter, and politeness, he couldn't charm Grandma Muse, who was suspicious of smooth talkers. "You'd have to be a saint to be married to her," Pa said.

Maybe Dad shook his head and smiled at how Pa spent his career in the auto industry but never drove a car, or how he loved baseball but never once played catch. Maybe he smelt his tobacco or heard his singing voice, distant, in his mind.

Maybe he wondered about his own kids, Janis and Joey, about his own mortality, about how far he had come since the days on Montlieu, about how much he was going to miss his father, how different life would be.

In 1956—one year before he died—Pa, sixty-nine, had been forced to retire from Chrysler. It deflated his pride. He viewed retirement as the step before death. He tended his garden with less vigor, he stopped going to Sunday ball games at Northwestern Field, and he no longer talked of moving out of the city to a farm like the one where he was raised in Poland.

"They're putting a race horse out to pasture," he said.

On an autumn Sunday, Teddy and Joe tried to lift his spirits. "Hey, Pa, let's go see the Lions game," Teddy suggested. (Detroit's football team then shared Briggs Stadium with the Tigers.)

"Nah," he said. "Don't feel like it."

They tried to convince him otherwise. But Pa, like his sons, was stubborn. He had been to the park two years earlier to see rookie outfielder Al Kaline. It was his final trip.

As a boy I embraced a simple caricature of the grandpa I never knew. On the one extreme there was fun-loving Teddy, the jovial gentleman of Montlieu Street. On the other, the short-fused father who hit his namesake too hard and too often. He loved roses and baseball and left the worries to his wife. As adults we come to realize that we're all too complex, too filled with contradictions and changing motivations, to be painted accurately through a series of anecdotes that by their very nature distort and exaggerate us. Just as TV highlights of yesterday's ball game don't capture its subtleties and nuances, a selection of moments can't summarize a person's life. The highlights never show the mundane, they show the memorable. We forget the ordinary times that better represent us.

I would love to travel back for a day to glimpse him, to complete the picture and sharpen the image. I yearn for a clearer sense of what traits he passed on to my father so I might understand the origin of those my father passed on to me. But, alas, it's not possible. There will always be questions unanswered.

Grandpa's mass was at Holy Name Church and Grandma was dressed in black, clenching rosary beads and praying for Pa's soul to be set free from purgatory.

It was a big funeral, with lots of roses.

◇ ◇ ◇ ◇ ◇ ◇ ◇   *The Kaline Encounter*

Al Kaline.
Photo
courtesy
of Burton
Historical
Collection,
Detroit
Public
Library.

**Game 38: Friday, June 18** ◇ Al Kaline is alone, reclining on the dugout bench and staring across the vacant infield toward the fence in right. The players are in the clubhouse and the gates haven't opened. It's pretty much Kaline over there, me over here, and a few grounds workers scattered about.

I've lived this moment since the opener in April; I've dreamt it since boyhood. And now it lays before me, too close to be a desert mirage.

As a writer you can imply things by stating a man is alone. You can suggest that he is absorbed in thought, lost in reflection, contemplative, nostalgic. That he is moody, remote, isolated, lonely, or lonesome. That he is waiting or being made to wait. You can make his aloneness symbolic, encouraging others to infer that he stands out, apart, has no rivals. What you hope, though, as you approach him is that he is alone merely because no one else has arrived and that he will welcome you.

Al Kaline sees me walking toward him. I am as self-conscious as a seventh-grader heading into the junior-high showers in September. He looks briefly and returns his eyes to the field. I sense him tightening as I sit. He doesn't speak.

"Mr. Kaline," I begin, drawing his attention. Men like Kaline have been interviewed thousands of times. A meeting like this one, shadowed by the possibility that I have upset his solitude, can falter early and never recover.

"Who are you with?" he asks.

I explain about the book and interpret the silence that follows as permission to continue.

"Father's Day is Sunday. I'd like to talk with you about fathers, sons, and baseball."

He waits.

"Did your dad play a role in your career?"

He pauses enough to make me notice, maybe wondering whether he wants to do this.

"If it wasn't for my father," he says finally, "I wouldn't have played baseball."

"You grew up in a row house in Baltimore, right?"

"Yep, about a mile and a half from Camden Yards."

Railroad tracks converged at Camden, two blocks from where Babe Ruth was born. It was also the city where Kaline's dad, Nicholas, and his dad's five brothers played, most as catchers.

"In downtown Baltimore there were just cement ball

fields," says Kaline. "There were no teams where I lived. All the semipro fields I played at we had to drive to. It was a lot of work for my father. He followed me around after he'd worked all day. He was a broom maker. He came to my games. I think he really enjoyed watching me. He also let me know I had responsibilities. Some days I wanted to go to the shore and swim. My father said I had a responsibility to the team."

The older Kaline, recognizing his only son's talent, encouraged him. "Try to learn everything you can about the game, try to be a complete ballplayer," he said.

"Not everybody played football and basketball," Kaline says. "Most everybody played baseball. It's something fathers can relate to with their sons."

In 1953 Kaline made the majors at eighteen. His parents came to Detroit occasionally and saw him when he visited their town. "Fortunately, in my early years I played there a lot against the Orioles and Washington Senators."

Twenty-one seasons later on September 24, 1974, his parents were at Memorial Stadium in his hometown of Baltimore when he doubled off Dave McNally for his three-thousandth hit, following Mays, Aaron, and Clemente into an elite, twelve-member club and ensuring his own baseball immortality.

I was thirteen. That weekend I went with a friend and his dad to Tiger Stadium on a day set aside to honor Kaline. They handed us posters as we entered the park. It was cold, the Tigers were in last place, and the only reason 20,000 fans showed up was to clap for him.

He looked weary at age thirty-nine, relegated to the role of designated hitter, a position created by God to ensure that Kaline would reach the magic plateau. He was past his prime but endowed with a dignity that accompanies true heroes no matter what their age. This was, after all, the man who in 1971 refused a pay increase because his batting average had dipped into the .270s. It was settling to see Kaline on the field each summer with the Old English *D* emblazoned on his left chest. Through race riots, through the assassinations of King and Kennedy, through Vietnam death counts on the morning news, through the crimes of our president, through Mom's many brain surgeries, through times of turmoil and uncertainty, he had been there, every season, and it meant something.

On that Sunday we stood and cheered his every at-bat. He got two hits and five standing ovations. We clapped as if the clapping should never end.

Now, these many years later, as our conversation winds down in the dugout where Gehringer and Greenberg sat before him—as he talks about his sons and four grandchildren, as he relates how his father, who died earlier this decade, encouraged him to become a broadcaster after his playing days because "he realized this is where I belong"—I'd like to tell him what he has meant to me. I'd like to tell him that even today I know his stats without checking the *Baseball Encyclopedia*: 3,007 hits, a .297 average, 399 home runs. And that I remember how he removed himself from the lineup of his final game, too humble to take that last bow.

"Thank you," I say, leaving him alone, and he thinks I'm talking about the interview.

—— **Detroit 8 ◇ Oakland 3** ——

Justin Thompson surrenders three hits in eight innings. Luis Polonia drives in three runs.

**Game 39: Saturday, June 19** ◇ The pilgrimages have begun already. With the home season almost half over, faraway fans have been coming to bid farewell to Tiger Stadium. A busload with Jay Buckley Tours rolled into Detroit this morning. On board was Jim Sandoval, an Alabama history teacher who has visited twenty-eight ballparks in five years.

"I had to come back to say good-bye to this shrine," he says. "There have been so many great players here. I can picture an outfield of Kaline, Cobb, and Crawford. I feel like I'm about to see the ghost of Cobb walking across the field. Here and Fenway—both give you that feeling."

Sandoval takes his baseball history more seriously than most. A member of the Society for American Baseball Research, he is documenting the 1919 Cincinnati Reds season play by play, convinced that the team would have won that year's World Series even if the Black Sox hadn't taken bribes to throw it.

Sandoval appreciates that the Sox of 1919 played on this field.

"What makes the old parks distinct are their features," he says. "I like the parks where at a glance you know where it is. If you fall asleep watching a TV game from Cincinnati and you wake up in the Pittsburgh or Philadelphia park, you wouldn't know. They are ashtray stadiums. Here it's like a living history museum. It'll still be the Tigers franchise at the new park but it won't be the same."

In the seats above Sandoval, Doug Brown Jr., eleven, holds a sign that reads, *The grass will always be greener at the corner of Michigan and Trumbull.* He came from London, Ontario.

"I think it's time for a change, like in Cleveland," he says. "But Tiger Stadium will never die. In the back of every Tiger fan's mind, they'll always have the memories."

—— **Oakland 13** ◇ **Detroit 1** ——

Oakland hammers five Detroit pitchers. Luis Polonia extends his hitting streak to fourteen games with four hits, raising his average to .443.

**Game 40: Sunday, June 20** ◇ It fits that Brian Moehler is pitching on Father's Day, dusting his dad's initials into the dirt.

"Maybe he'll throw a no-hitter," says Mike Varney, once more passing through from Milwaukee. "It would be as if his father called one in from upstairs."

As fathers and sons, we find comfort in that thought. Mike's dad, Sonny, died in 1983; my mom in 1996. The notion that those who once watched over us continue to watch over us makes their deaths more bearable.

We're up high in the right-field deck, no one near us on this afternoon, with the temperature in the 70s and the sun glistening on the grass. A warm breeze sweeps through the stands.

We talk about our kids.

Mike has a daughter, Thea, and a son he named for Kirk Gibson. Like Taylor and William, Kirk plays league baseball. Also like them, he has passions that lie elsewhere. Our boys differ from us in that respect, which of course is fine. Kirk loves art. For William it's music; for Taylor, movies. Zack, who came to the park yesterday for a belated birthday celebration with friends, savors politics. He watches C-Span and dreams of being a congressional page, as I dreamt of being a batboy.

By the third inning Brian Moehler has given up hits and runs. No help from the heavens or elsewhere appears to be on the way.

On this Father's Day my dad is with my brother and sisters and their families. He understands about me being here and he's warming to the idea of a reunion with his brothers, should it be possible. He's been reminiscing more lately, which I enjoy. He has planted doubts about whether Uncle Tom will actually come to a game. "He used to cancel out at the last minute," Dad said. "We'd invite them over for dinner and he'd call to say they wouldn't be coming." With Uncle Herb, we both doubt that he'll make it over from Asia for a ball game. Besides, Mike has had no luck locating him.

"I haven't heard anything," he says before I ask.

—— **Oakland 6 ◇ Detroit 5** ——

Despite an eighth-inning grand slam by Dean Palmer, his nineteenth home run, the Tigers lose their fifth in six games.

**Game 41: Monday, June 21 ◇** Ken Griffey Jr. didn't sign Pete Munoz's magazine. He didn't sign the photo of him leaping for a ball in front of Pete.

"To hell with him," Pete says in the bleachers. "He made me mad."

Pete's eyes are red, maybe from too little sleep. He pledges that he's going to put the word *Asshole* on the back of his Griffey jersey.

"I told him, 'Hey, that's me in the picture,' " he says. Griffey kept walking.

It's the first evening of summer and the setting sun throws a column of red light onto a section of the third deck. My journey has crossed the halfway point. The days sail by.

Near first base Matt Wojcik, angrier than I over the closing of this park, vows to honor this place in a way that could land him in jail. His friends try to discourage him. He promises to fill me in later.

—— **Detroit 13** ◇ **Oakland 11** ——

Dean Palmer belts his ninth homer in fourteen games, his twentieth of the season, third-best in the league. Tony Clark provides the winning run in the eighth inning.

◇ ◇ ◇ ◇ ◇ ◇ ◇   *The Submarine Pitcher*

Elden Auker, submarine pitcher. Photo courtesy of Burton Historical Collection, Detroit Public Library.

**Game 42: Friday, June 25** ◇ I have put on ten pounds in two months and it's no mystery. In my right hand, swabbed with mustard, awaits the uneaten half of a hot dog, my twenty-odd one of the season.

You can eat only so many ballpark hot dogs before they start to taste like ordinary hot dogs and before you start to wonder what it was about them that once appealed to you. Soon you find yourself thinking about their fleshy color, their too-smooth consistency, the circular pattern of the meat, and even their tubular shape.

You can think too much about a hot dog.

But the contest alone no longer holds your interest, not

when it's between two of the worst clubs, not when your team is hopelessly out of the race.

When I was fourteen and the '75 Tigers were mired in last place on their way to their poorest record in twenty years, I could convince myself we still had a chance. If Mickey Lolich, Joe Coleman, and Bill Freehan could play like they used to; if manager Ralph Houk would put Ben Oglivie in the lineup every day; if right fielder Leon Roberts could hit like Kaline; if . . .

Anymore, I don't bother with "if"s.

—— **Detroit 2** ◇ **Minnesota 0** ——

Brian Moehler tosses the team's first complete game, a six-hitter. Dean Palmer knocks in both runs.

**Game 43: Saturday, June 26** ◇ In the third inning the scoreboard scrolls a list of fans celebrating wedding anniversaries. Beth spots our names. She tilts her head toward my shoulder, her blue eyes dancing. We've been married sixteen years but have never celebrated our anniversary at the stadium. Until we met, Beth had never been to the park. I introduced her to baseball; she introduced me to Pete Seeger, blue herons, and William Morris tapestries.

When I told an acquaintance about my plan to see all eighty-one home games, he rolled his eyes. "Your real story," he said, "will be how your marriage survives it."

He doesn't know Beth.

Four summers ago we went to England. We spent a week in Grasmere, a pretty lakeside village in the rural north, in a stone cottage called Howthwaite. I awoke one morning to her silhouette in the bedroom window, where she sat, wrapped in a quilt, with a hot cup of Earl Grey in her palms and the window open and the scent of lavender and rhododendrons on the breeze and the green hillside in the distance with slate paths and sheep in the meadow far below. And she was crying.

"What's wrong?"

"I absolutely love it here," she said. "I feel like I've come home."

Beth had visited Britain once before—"once before in this life," she would say. She felt a deep attachment, an affection that couldn't be explained. She is that way about places and she understands my need to be here.

—— Minnesota 1 ◇ Detroit 0 ——

Dave Mlicki pitches well but loses.

**Game 44: Sunday, June 27** ◇ The weather, drizzly and overcast, forces the ball club to hold Photo Day in the covered concourse behind the left-field stands. Fans move in a long line, shooting flash pictures as they pass Tigers perched on stools behind a rope.

It's an odd setup because they can't see the names on the uniforms. Though some are recognizable—tall Tony Clark, Japanese pitcher Masao Kida, muscular Gabe Kapler—many look like generic ballplayers, extras in a movie.

Two pitchers, Todd Jones and Doug Brocail, set their stools in front of the rope to be closer to fans. Jones hoists little ones onto his lap without having to be asked and invites high-fives from older kids.

"You playing today?" asks a boy about ten.

"Every day!" says Jones, who as a reliever never knows in advance.

More kids wear Bobby Higginson jerseys than those of any player, but Higginson isn't grinning for cameras. He's on the field with Alan Trammell; they're working on his swing. Higginson has struggled with one hit in twenty-two at-bats, a disappointment for the veteran who was supposed to be at the heart of the order. Trade talks spin around him.

In the Tiger Room after finishing eggs scrambled with jalapeño peppers, broadcaster Ernie Harwell notices I am alone and takes the seat next to me.

"Where do you live?" he asks, biting into a strawberry.

We talk about small towns and weather and traffic on the freeway and he says he prefers radio work to television—"too many gadgets with TV; too much can go wrong." He enjoys traveling with the team and he's having a blast being back full-time. He says it would be best for the neighborhood if the city demolished Tiger Stadium after the team leaves. He fears, otherwise, that the park will sit empty and fall into disrepair, a bulky reminder of better days, an impediment to the people who live around here in the present, not the past. And then he's off to the radio booth.

On the field a commotion stirs near home plate. At the center of it is a man I don't recognize. He's tall, over six feet, and straight-backed for his age. He walks to the mound as if he's done it a hundred times before. I miss his introduction. But when he pulls back his right arm and delivers the ceremonial first pitch—underhand, submarine style—it strikes me. Instantly I'm a kid of eleven and Dad has come home from work at the tank plant. It's four in the afternoon and I've been waiting.

"Will you play catch with me?" I ask.

"In a minute," he always says.

Soon he's in the shade of the birch tree with his steel-toed shoes still on, wearing my extra mitt, the George Scott first-baseman's model.

Dad is fifty-two with modest sideburns and receding black hair. His belly edges over his belt.

"I think Eddie Brinkman's way better than Mark Belanger, don't you?"

"Brinkman's good," he says, sounding like he agrees. "Billy Rogell was a good one, too, and Harvey Kuenn."

I reach back and throw as hard as I can, imagining myself Nolan Ryan, the California Angel who seemed to come out of nowhere that summer. Dad listens to me chatter about baseball, occasionally adding a few words.

"Tommy, you've got a one-track mind," he says, and I take it as a compliment.

For twenty minutes he throws soft grounders and looping pop-ups that I try to turn into diving catches. He handles my throws with a smooth sweep that flows into a gentle, rocking windup. He returns the ball underhand.

"Submarine style," he says. "That's how Elden Auker did it."

Dad explains that Auker developed the delivery after a shoulder injury ended his days as a college quarterback. He could no longer pitch overhand so he adapted. He won eighteen games for the world champion Tigers of 1935, when Dad was fifteen.

And now in June 1999 Auker is on the field again, eighty-eight years old, and throwing an underhand pitch that bounces near the plate. But all I see is my dad and I have to dry my eyes.

Finally it's starting to make sense.

––––– **Minnesota 12  ◊  Detroit 7** –––––

Jeff Weaver, the first of seven Detroit pitchers, gives up seven runs in less than two innings.

**Game 45: Tuesday, July 6** ◇ "Paulie sucks! Paulie sucks! Paulie sucks!"

Teens in the lower bleachers are chanting at Yankee star Paul O'Neill.

"You six-million-dollar wuss."

John Lee Davids, the architect who tried to save Tiger Stadium, shakes his head from his bench a few rows up.

"The time to heckle a guy isn't when he has a double and two RBIs," he says, amused.

New York players evoke strong feelings in Detroit. The rivalry dates to the clashes of Cobb and Ruth, players of different eras who despised each other and brawled on this field.

How sad that this series should be the final Tiger Stadium matchup between these two teams. The season is barely half over and already New York, which played in this park its first year, is bidding farewell. It's disappointing. September should be stacked with home games against Boston, Cleveland, and Chicago, teams that visited in 1912. Instead we'll close against Kansas City, a 1969 expansion team. Heck, I've been around longer than the Royals.

For Davids, the architect, it won't matter who the Tigers play on September 27.

"I decided not to come," he says. "I don't like how the Tigers marketed it."

Over the past decade the ball club has decried the condition of the current park and pushed for a new one. This year, though, officials played heavily on nostalgia and history to sell tickets. They promoted season packages as the only way to guarantee seats at the closing game. Davids wasn't about to buy into the scheme.

He's not happy with much about this year, starting with the fact that it is the final one. He says that Ernie Harwell disappointed him and that Detroit sports reporters showed themselves "to be a bunch of cement heads."

"Joe Falls would flip and flop every few weeks," he says. Don't even ask about the two mayors and various team officials.

"I was naive to think we would win," he says. "But it was something worth doing. We bought about five years of life for the park. At least I got a chance to bring my kids here."

—— **New York 9 ◇ Detroit 8** ——

Bobby Higginson ties the game in the ninth on a home run. The Yankees win in the tenth.

◇ ◇ ◇ ◇ ◇ ◇   *Johnny Castiglione*

Some Club Crusader members, including
Johnny Castiglione and Dad in the back row.

**Game 46: Wednesday, July 7** ◇ Several women
wave poster-board proposals behind the New York dugout.

*Derek Jeter, will you marry this gal from Kalamazoo?* says
one. Jeter played high-school ball in central Michigan.

In the fourth inning he triples off the left-field wall in front
of Dad, Zack, and me. We're behind the home-run fence, next
to the yellow pole that separates fair territory from foul.

"Dad," says Zack, "if you picked an all-Michigan team,
who would be on it?" He quickly nominates Jeter as shortstop
and John Smoltz as pitcher.

"Willie Horton, Bill Freehan," I add.

"Hal Newhouser," says my dad, recalling his sandlot nemesis. "Charlie Gehringer. Barney McCosky—wasn't he from here?"

"How about an all-Yankee team?" Zack asks. He takes Ruth, Mantle, DiMaggio, and Gehrig. "Who would be at second and short?"

"Lazzeri and Rizzuto," Dad says.

I'm sitting in the middle. No empty seats between us. It's nighttime, the big lights are on, and the Tigers are ahead for a change. Not that it matters much. They're already twenty games out of first and fifteen games under .500. They have as much chance as McGovern did in 1972. Absent a miracle, their season is over—with seventy-eight games to go. Which doesn't explain why 25,000 fans have come out. It's a good turnout for a weeknight. Even George Steinbrenner, owner of the Yankees, has shown. It's the park. Everybody wants to see the park to say good-bye.

I'm doing it all season.

"I don't have no attachments to places," Dad says for no apparent reason, and this surprises me. Does he realize the weight of these words to the son who is devoting most of a year to honoring this stadium, a mere place? "No attachments"? It's because of him I feel attached to this park.

Then he tells me about Johnny Castiglione, his childhood friend who during the Depression collected bits of coal that fell from railroad cars near Montlieu Street. Johnny took the coal home to his father and they used it to heat their house.

A few days ago Dad spotted Johnny's death notice in the paper. Dad showed up at the funeral home Monday. They had been friends since the 1930s. For as long as Dad can remember, Johnny had had one short leg, the result of polio.

"He really pitched unorthodox. But boy, could he pitch," he says. "Me and your uncle Ted would have to play in on the corners because teams would try to bunt on him and he couldn't get off the mound fast enough. He was a hell of a pitcher."

Over the years Johnny would surface at our house, a hefty man with a big limp and a left shoe with an enormous stacked sole, and he and Dad would get to talking about guys from the neighborhood and games long ago. After a Stroh's or two Johnny would complain that some guys never had wanted him to play ball.

"You always made me part of the team, Joe," he'd say.

Dad would drop his head slightly to the right, allowing the compliment to slide past him. "Well, you were a good pitcher, John," he would counter. And that would be as close as they'd get to hugging.

As teens Johnny and Dad had belonged to Club Crusader, a social group central to the lives of boys who lived around Montlieu Street. I've seen the club scrapbook at Dad's home, with pictures of Uncle Ted (they called him "Teets"), Lips, Glowicki, Konczal, and Kahanak—young men with attitude in their eyes. There's one photo of Johnny playing ice hockey in his bulky street shoes. Everyone else has skates.

The Crusaders wore reversible jackets, each sponsored by a different business. One side was gray, the other satiny purple. "The satin side was the dress side, with a big C," Dad explains. "Everybody envied those."

They played football, hockey, and fast-pitch softball, and they hosted parties.

"Johnny always said if he could, he'd go back to that period of time. That was the happiest time in his life."

Retired from Chrysler, Johnny drove to the neighborhood late at night when he couldn't sleep. He'd drive down Montlieu, Molena, and Mt. Olivet, and stop for coffee on Van Dyke.

"Your uncle Ted used to tell him, 'You live in the past.' And he'd say, 'Yes, and I love it. I'd give all my tomorrows for one yesterday.' He called me probably two months before he died. He was in a home. I said I'd drop over and he said, 'Naw.' He didn't want me to. He was on a dialysis machine. He said, 'When I feel like talking, I'll give you a call.' He wouldn't give me his telephone number, either. That was very unusual for John. He was very talkative. He always had time for people, knew everybody, and had a memory I wish I had. He could remember stuff when we were teenagers. Later on in life he looked up all his old girlfriends. Some were close to seventy. If they had died, he'd go visit their graves. He loved that time."

A bit of silence drifts between his words.

"I don't have no attachments to places," Dad says. "I'm more attached with people."

—— **Detroit 6** ◇ **New York 4** ——

Joe Torre.

**Game 47: Thursday, July 8** ◇ Joe Torre tucks his fingers in the front of his gray Yankee slacks, encircled by fourteen reporters who toss questions about the American League All-Star team, which he will manage. Shortstop Derek Jeter, fiddling at the bat rack nearby, interrupts the interview.

"Mr. Torre, are you going to miss the small dugouts at Tiger Stadium?" Jeter asks, impersonating a journalist.

"It's not as bad as in Boston," Torre says. "There's going to be a certain amount of charm you lose walking into a Fenway and a Tiger Stadium. But the dugout situation and clubhouse—there's not as much charm as in the stands."

Paul O'Neill might argue that there is no charm in the

stands. When he takes right field, O'Neill spots several young men with diapers on their heads. They shake baby bottles at him.

"You're a crybaby, Paula," one hollers.

Two games ago, after suffering chants of "your wife is a slut," O'Neill complained to the media. Inspired by the attention, vocal teens occupy the lower bleachers today.

Jeremy Price, Ryan Erskine, and Matt Hand have come to five of six Yankee games and they've been riding O'Neill every time. Yesterday a Tiger representative asked that they stop using the word "suck."

"We used to yell 'wife beater' at Albert Belle and we'd get no reaction," says Price. "Look at O'Neill's batting average when he comes to Detroit."

"We're taking him off his game," says Hand.

"He's like a really good player and he doesn't do well here," says Erskine.

The guys admit this is their entertainment.

"It costs $5 to see a Tiger game," notes Price. "You can't see a movie that cheap."

A few rows behind them, Alex Zapata, eight, endures the taunting. Alex and his family drove from Toledo, Ohio. His dad, Jesse, has been following O'Neill since his days as a Red. This afternoon Jesse caught two batting-practice balls and got O'Neill to sign one. He gave it to Alex.

"Paul O'Neill's the best," says the boy.

—— **New York 3** ◇ **Detroit 2** ——

Jeff Weaver completes eight innings and leaves with a tie after 111 pitches. Tino Martinez homers in the ninth. Weaver's winless streak hits eight games.

**Game 48: Friday, July 9** ◇ Paws has been gagged. The team mascot has been barred from speaking to me. The news came from the club's public-relations department this week. I'm reminded of it because Paws is strutting on the dugout in front of me.

"Paws doesn't do speaking engagements," I was informed in serious tones.

"Technically it would be an interview, not a speaking engagement," I said.

"Well, Paws does not speak."

"You mean I can interview Al Kaline, Mark McGwire, and Joe Torre, but not Paws?"

"Sorry," she said. "Oh, and Paws is a woman."

John and Jean Toutenhoofd, both in their fifties, aren't impressed by our mascot.

"He's no Bernie Brewer," says Jean. They're from Wisconsin, where Bernie slides into a mug of beer every time a Milwaukee player hits a home run.

For as much fun as they're having, it's difficult to imagine that in 1996 the Toutenhoofds nearly abandoned the sport they've followed since childhood. They became infuriated when Baltimore second baseman Roberto Alomar spit on umpire John Herschbeck and the league postponed Alomar's suspension, making him eligible for post-season play.

"Baseball is America and the umpire is authority," says Jean, a nurse. "In school if you didn't like your teachers and principals, you had to respect them. When kids see an overpaid person doing that to authority"—her voice trails off in rediscovered anger—"that's a bad standard to set. How do you expect kids to be of a better demeanor when their heroes are acting that way?"

John wrote Bud Selig, interim baseball commissioner and Brewers owner, and cancelled their season-ticket order. "A public-relations letter—that's all I was expecting," he says. Instead Selig called twice and left messages before reaching him on the third attempt. They talked for forty-five minutes about misbehavior by sports stars.

"Alomar should have been punished much more severely," says John, a social worker. "At least, he should have been barred from post-season play. All these players are heroes to kids."

Though they respected Selig for his concern, the Toutenhoofds allowed their tickets to expire. "It killed me not going to baseball as much as we were used to," says Jean, offering me red licorice that she brought from home.

Meanwhile manager Larry Parrish gets booed for removing reliever Will Brunson after he retires two hitters. Parrish's pitching coach, Rick Adair, was dismissed yesterday.

"They should have fired you," yells one man.

—— **Milwaukee 4** ◇ **Detroit 1** ——

Brewer Jeromy Burnitz lifts one over the right-field roof, the season's third out-of-the-park home run.

**Game 49: Saturday, July 10** ◇ Two members of an oldies rock band exit a long autograph line talking about the tanned guy with curly hair.

"I remember Ernie Harwell saying that they hadn't seen anybody like him since Babe Ruth," recalls Tom Driscoll.

Dennis Hafeli nods. "He's genuine."

For one season, the Bicentennial summer of '76, Mark Fidrych enthralled the baseball world. He danced about the diamond like a hopped-up caffeine addict, spoke to the ball, and manicured the mound on his knees. "The Bird" forced a fifth-place team into the national spotlight. He started the All-Star game and he packed the stands en route to winning Rookie of the Year. But the glory was brief. His career crashed with a series of injuries and his short reign as the sport's most popular player fizzled too soon, a disappointment bigger than comet Kohoutek.

Fidrych also contributed to my most-doomed adolescent experiment. It was the spring of my sixteenth year, early 1977, when my older sister offered to make me look like Mark Fidrych.

"Girls like guys with curly hair," she said.

I consented and she bound my hair in rollers and doused it with chemicals that burned my scalp and pierced my sinuses. I hoped that my rolling locks would lure Don Addington's girlfriend, whose hair feathered back in Farrah Fawcett loveliness. My plan failed, though. I did not resemble Fidrych—not even Peter Frampton. I looked like Gene Shalit, and Addington's girl would have nothing to do with me.

Fidrych is forty-four. He still possesses the unassuming nature that prompted thousands to send him money in 1976 because they felt the Tigers were taking advantage of his "Gomer Pyle" goodness by paying him the major-league minimum of $20,000 while he was selling millions in tickets.

On the road that year he roomed with a veteran. After Fidrych's debut—a two-hitter against Cleveland—Joe Coleman told him, "Roomie, don't sit on your first victory." Coleman bought him shaving cream and persuaded him to clean up.

"He was guiding me. He was like a mom, except he was a guy," says Fidrych.

The rookie won seven of his first eight starts, all by one run.

He headed into the June 28, 1976, contest with a six-game winning streak. That game against the Yankees on *Monday Night Baseball* altered his life.

Fidrych drove into the city with his neighbor, shortstop Tommy Veryzer, and they spotted the masses of people outside the park. "Tommy said, 'They're here to see you,' " Fidrych recalls. "I said, 'No, they're here to see the team.' He said, 'They're here to see just you.' In the clubhouse Vern Ruhle said the same thing; Steve Kemp, too. They kept me relaxed. That was probably one of the biggest games in my life. My family was seeing it. It was in Massachusetts [on TV]; it was *Monday Night Baseball*. . . . The outcome was picture-written."

Fidrych beat the Yankees 5–1.

"It didn't change me," he says. "It changed my life. Everyone knew me, coast to coast. I was only twenty-one."

By age twenty-five his career was over. Fidrych, though, doesn't curse his injuries.

"It's part of an athlete's life. You get hurt," he says. "If you want depression, go to Ford Hospital in the children's ward. I'm fortunate. I'm a lucky guy. I made it to the big leagues. I made it to the final spot. No one can take that away. It's a wishing that I've always wanted."

Fidrych owns a Massachusetts farm—a "gennleman's fahh-hhmm," he calls it—a place where children pet goats and milk cows. He lives there with his wife and their twelve-year-old daughter Jessica. It augments his income hauling concrete in a ten-wheeler.

Fidrych has tried to explain the magic of that first summer to his daughter. She was unimpressed until a few years ago when he pulled out the cover of an outdated *Sports Illustrated*. It featured Fidrych, and Big Bird of *Sesame Street*.

"You know Big Bird?" she asked, astonished.

"What happened in '76, it was big," he says now. "I didn't realize how big."

—— **Detroit 9 ◇ Milwaukee 3** ——

Seven Tigers knock in runs, led by Bobby Higginson with three hits. Justin Thompson throws a five-hitter over eight innings.

**Game 50: Sunday, July 11 ◇** On a weekday in 1927, the year Charles Lindbergh would fly solo to Paris, Fred Smith got out of school at one-thirty, plowed through his *Detroit News* paper route, and rushed to Navin Field, where for the first time he saw an afternoon ball game by himself.

"Do I remember it?" he says, his jolly voice rising. "I was the first in the ballpark. It was an ordinary game. A Thursday. I come in and there's a ball on the ground in the bleachers. A little while later when the ballplayers were out there, I asked this White Sox player for a ball and he gave it to me. Next thing, I asked him if he would autograph it. I tossed it back, he signed it: Ted Lyons.

"Then came the big thrill," says Smith. "Just before the last ball was thrown in, there's Heinie Manush. 'Heinie has no business out here'—that was my expression. It stuck with Heinie forever. 'No business here, kid?' Anyway, I got the ball. From then on I got baseballs galore. Heinie gave me a baseball every game I went. When he was traded, he went to St. Louis. When he went into the Hall of Fame in Cooperstown, I was there. Had dinner with him the night before. He still called me 'kid'."

On his 1927 solo adventure Smith had met two future Hall of Famers; it was only the beginning. At the ballpark, then as now, the clubhouse emptied into the concourse, meaning that players couldn't leave without passing through fans. Smith always waited. He met Babe Ruth—"he was nice to everybody"—and Lou Gehrig—"kind of aloof." He met Earl Whitehill, a handsome pitcher who married a raisin-box model.

"He was a hothead," he says. "He'd get mad when an infielder blew one. After the game he was always nice to the kids. Even if he got blown out of the ballpark, he was still there."

The encounter he best remembers involved Ty Cobb. Smith lived blocks from Cobb's home at Burlingame and Second. "I used to go over by his house all the time. I'd stand out there a long time. But I never saw him."

Smith cornered Cobb outside the clubhouse. By then Cobb was playing for Philadelphia. "He told me to be good in school, like you would do any kid. He signed a ball for me. He was beautiful. Wonderful. It always made me mad when you'd read these stories about how miserable he was because these guys who wrote about him never saw him. They weren't alive when he was playing. It was one of the great thrills of my life, and I'm eighty-two."

Smith learned to sneak into games. Copying the method of an older kid, he identified himself as "a friend of Mr. O'Keefe."

"Go on in, son," the usher would say. O'Keefe tended bar at a speakeasy and every time Smith went in, the usher redeemed the favor for a beer.

"The greatest game I ever saw was against the Yankees in 1950," says Smith, sipping a soda in the media dining room. "We were fighting for the pennant. Teddy Gray starts for us and Tommy Byrne is on the mound for the Yankees. Byrne was tough. They were ahead 6–0. Gray comes out of there. We come up to bat in the fourth or fifth inning."

By this point others in the room are listening to Smith.

"Trout is batting with the bases loaded and hits a home run. It's 6–4. Lipon goes out, then Jerry Priddy hits a home run, 6–5. Kell singles. Wertz homers, 7–6. Evers homers, 8–6. In the ninth inning they're ahead 9–8. Wertz or Kell doubles and Evers gets an inside-the-park home run.

"You remember that, don't you, John?" Smith says to John Allgeyer, a stadium worker.

"I was at that game," Allgeyer says.

"That was the greatest game you ever saw, wasn't it?"

"Oh yeah."

"There was no one who saw that game who wouldn't remember it," Smith says. "Oh, it was hotter than Kelsey's raft out there that night. What a ball game."

Smith shakes his head at the memory. He has seen more than a thousand games at the park, from dozens of home openers to All-Star games and the World Series. When you hit forty or fifty games a year over several decades, you get to be a familiar face. The ushers get to know you. The officials and the players, too. It happened with Fred Smith. So, when he retired early from the insurance business in the mid-1970s, the Tigers asked him to handle group-ticket sales.

He wrote trivia books with Ernie Harwell and Brooks Robinson, had a small business venture with Al Kaline, and drove an elderly Charlie Gehringer to ball games. But one of his favorite men was Lynn Jones, a little-known fourth out-fielder who played five seasons through 1983.

"I used to take boys into the clubhouse because every one of those kids was me when I was ten," says Smith. "Lynn Jones would come and see me. He would find out the boy's name and come up and say, 'Is this Steve Stewart? Steve, I heard you were coming down and I wanted to meet you.'

Well, that kid would beam from here to Niagara Falls. I always had a special fondness for Jones because of that."

Smith and I head out of the dining room into the concourse as the game is about to start. He stops as the National Anthem plays. He taps the shoulder of the boy in front of him.

"Take off your hat," he says.

Smith sings loudly, slightly off-tune, and ahead of the performer. As the song ends, the boy puts his cap back on.

"I like people," Smith says. "Unfortunately, after you retire, life is for the birds. All your friends are gone. I had a lot of friends and they're all buried. Not all of them, but most of them. I can't read anymore. I read, I get tired, and I fall asleep. Consequently, watching the ball games, I don't watch them as seriously as I used to. For years I kept score at every game. I don't approve of a lot of the things they've done. I don't like the designated hitter. I don't like interleague play. I don't like fifteen teams in a league. It's not the same game."

His age tempers his sadness about the closing of the park where he has spent his life.

"Everything comes to an end," Smith says. "I've seen so many of my friends pass away. Everything comes to an end, you know. Friendships you've had here and there. It's part of life. We lived in a house in Southfield for twenty-eight years. We moved four years ago. I still drive by and wave at it because I love that house. My wife wanted to move and I didn't. She was right. But I still love that house. My daughters grew up in it.

"Memories—they stick," he says. "I'm a sentimentalist. I'm going to feel badly about the ballpark. But everything comes to an end."

—— **Milwaukee 3** ◇ **Detroit 2** ——

The Tigers head into the All-Star break sixteen games under .500 and twenty games out of first. Larry Parrish tells his team to view the second half of the year as a new season.

◇ ◇ ◇ ◇ ◇ ◇ ◇   *Dreams and Nightmares*

Briggs Stadium, 1950s. Photo courtesy of
Burton Historical Collection, Detroit Public Library.

**Game 51: Wednesday, July 21** ◇ The outfield
looks like a sickly squirrel, its coat bare in spots. Four days
ago, with the Tigers on the road, the Three Tenors—Pavarotti,
Domingo, and Carreras—packed the stadium. The weight of
the elaborate outfield stage and temporary, on-field seating
left grounds chief Heather Nabozny with a nightmare: an
uneven landscape, compacted grass, and frayed turf.

Outside the park that concert night, Matt Wojcik, not
wanting to spring for a pricey ticket, wandered along Michigan and Trumbull. Music wafted over the streets. He walked
beside the gray-sided building and thought about his allegiance to this place. He recalled hugging the park years ago

when thousands protested the proposal to abandon it. He remembered driving past it last winter to see it in the snow, and he pondered the secret plan that could get him arrested.

John Ward and Tom Willard know about it. The three have been friends since their days at Anchor Bay High School in the late 1980s. I've known Tom for ten years; he used to work for my newspapers. At tonight's game, Wojcik, who has the tight features of a wooden puppet, talks once again about how he wants to hide in the seats and sleep in the park.

"I'll probably do it after a Friday-night game after the fireworks," he says. "Maybe I'll see the ghost of Ty Cobb or Harry Heilmann. I've always wanted to do it. I've got to do it this year."

Ward smirks. "You're demented. Don't call me for bail money, all right?"

"We're not going to get caught," Wojcik snaps. "There are so many nooks and crannies, you could live in here and nobody would know it."

When Wojcik, twenty-eight, talks about the park's final season, he becomes a revival-tent preacher who believes city and ball-club officials will go to hell for perpetrating an unforgivable sin.

"There's never going to be another Tiger Stadium," he says. "It's much, much more than cement. It's Detroit. It's a shrine. In that movie *Tiger Town*, the guy says, 'Kid, they'll never tear this place down.' Well, they're going to tear it down."

After this season, Wojcik vows, he will become a Chicago Cubs fan. He says he will make the five-hour drive to Wrigley Field for a team that appreciates its history. He has pledged not to buy tickets to Comerica Park.

"I don't want any part of it."

"Well, I'll be there," says Ward.

"You never have a cause," Wojcik replies.

"You're just bitter because you're never on the winning side."

"Draw a line in the sand."

"Every time you pick a cause, you pick the losing end. You're always getting crushed."

"Who wins against corporate America? Nobody!"

Willard laughs.

"They fight over everything," he says. "'Woj' is the traditionalist; John is the progressive. There's no middle ground."

Wojcik sips his beer.

"Some fan has to spend a night here," he says, his mission taking shape.

—— **Detroit 10 ◇ Kansas City 5** ——

Tony Clark, emerging from a slump, puts the Tigers ahead with a three-run blast, his fifth in six games.

**Game 52: Thursday, July 22** ◇ The Detroit players have returned to the clubhouse, except for rookie pitcher Dave Borkowski, who's alone on the dugout bench forty-five minutes before the game. He sits still, so still that you know he's trying to harness his racing mind and contain his nerves and focus his thoughts and fool himself into being calm. He stares straight ahead, eyes like a stunned deer.

This may be the biggest day of his life, and Borkowski, twenty-two, feels it. Called up last week, he is minutes from his first appearance at the stadium. Here as a boy he dreamed of somedays.

Borkowski came six hours early yesterday, driving thirty-five minutes from his parents' suburban home where he lives.

He beat his teammates to the park. It was his first visit as a uniformed club member. "I knew my time was running out to get a shot to pitch here," he said. "It means a lot. I've grown up watching the Tigers. It's been a dream to step out on that mound at least for a game. I knew this is what I wanted to do and where I wanted to play. I came here a bunch of times to watch baseball games. I just kind of sat there, watched, and soaked it in."

Borkowski graduated in 1995 from Sterling Heights High School, the same school I attended seventeen years earlier. It is a monolithic structure with windowless classrooms.

"Going into high school I thought I had a realistic chance at being drafted and getting a shot. It's always been my dream. I kind of liked the way Jack Morris went about his business. I liked that he was a hard-nosed, aggressive, intense pitcher. I like to think I'm similar."

On this sweaty afternoon when shirts stick to skin, the announcer introduces the local kid—"warming up in the bullpen, today's starting pitcher, Dave Borkowski"—and applause erupts. Two hundred family members, coaches, and neighborhood pals have come to support him.

"Go get him, Davey," says one man. Behind the plate a boy wears a Borkowski jersey and four young ladies lift a homemade sign that reads, *Dave, you've come a long way, baby!*

Cheers usher Borkowski into the game. But he walks the leadoff hitter and goes high in the count to the next. One batter flies deep to right, one singles. It's a shaky start and he is lucky to escape without surrendering a run. Borkowski charges to the dugout, snapping the cap from his head in frustration.

It will be a rough day: five runs, four walks, and nine hits in less than six innings.

—— **Detroit 9 ◇ Kansas City 8** ——

**Game 53: Friday, July 23** ◇ An afternoon storm rolls in and blows several panels off the exterior of the press box, closing the seating sections below and delaying the game fifty minutes. In another era this game might be postponed and a doubleheader scheduled for tomorrow. Anymore, baseball has an aversion to giving fans two games for the price of one. Besides, with over 38,000 tickets sold and many of their holders on hand, it would be an unpopular decision. Instead the teams play on wet turf, and left fielder Juan Encarnacion chases a foul ball, skids eight feet on slippery grass, falls awkwardly, and injures his right ankle. He gets carted away.

In the stands my boys order three-dollar Cokes from Tiger Den waitresses.

"Hey, can you guys name the Tiger Hall of Famers?" I point to the third deck in right-field foul territory, where placards display the last names of twelve Detroit inductees. My boys identify Ty Cobb, Al Kaline, and Ernie Harwell. Zack also gets Charlie Gehringer and Hank Greenberg.

"Who's Cochrane?" he asks.

I tell them that Mickey Cochrane caught and managed the city's first world championship team. But they're more interested in how his playing career ended in June 1937 with a ball that beaned him above the ear. The near-fatal pitch left him unconscious for ten days. He returned to manage but was never the same. "Your grandpa Joe says that when Cochrane would catch, you could hear him jabbering behind the plate at the other players. In those days they didn't play loud music before each batter."

I work through the rest of the list: Sam Crawford, who hit more triples than any player in history; Harry Heilmann, whose .342 lifetime average was as good as Babe Ruth's; George Kell, a ten-time All-Star; Heinie Manush, who succeeded Cobb in center; Hughie Jennings, the impassioned manager who handled Cobb skillfully; and Hal Newhouser. "You remember: Grandpa Joe batted against him."

"Oh, right," says Zack. " 'King Hal.' "

" 'Prince Hal.' "

"Whatever."

In the coming days Zack will head to camp with his baritone and his high-school marching band. To his horror I'll be there as a chaperon, jangling the coins in my pocket.

—— **Detroit 14** ◇ **Boston 5** ——

Shortstop Deivi Cruz knocks in four runs. He has raised his average forty points, to over .270. The Tigers have won five of their last six.

**Game 54: Saturday, July 24** ◇ I am at the park two and a half hours early. It is the time I enjoy most—before the game, before the crowd, before I have to share this place with thousands. Behind me a forklift motors along the concourse, beeping as it carries supplies to concession stands. On the field, manager Larry Parrish crouches to the left of his fifteen-year-old son Joshua and tosses a ball underhand. Joshua slaps it into a net. Nearer the dugout, hot-hitting Luis Polonia watches Bianca, his daughter, balance a bat in the palm of her hand. The most unusual sight, though, is Bill Eisner, the photographer. He's in the batting cage, having convinced bullpen coach Jeff Jones to pitch to him.

"Keep your elbow up," Jones says.

Eisner has a rusty softball swing. His best hit makes it to second base and he's happy.

This has been a gratifying week. I phoned my uncle Tom's daughter, whom I've seen twice in my life, to enlist her help in getting our fathers together at the ballpark. (I tried Uncle Tom first but got an answering machine.) She liked the idea; I had thought she might. Nine years back, she had spotted the obituary for our uncle Teddy in the newspaper; though she had never met him—nor any of the family—she suspected that he might be a relative and she showed up at the funeral, paying her respects anonymously. Anyway, she called her father and he called me. It was much easier than I anticipated. No pauses or pondering, just a joyous yes. In August Uncle Tom and Dad will come together at Tiger Stadium. That's the plan, at least. I told Dad and he's thrilled but cautious. "We'll see if it happens," he said.

Before today's game, four generations of the Briggs family gather behind home plate for a photo. "We decided it was very necessary to come this year," says Walter Briggs III, vice president of a Northeast investment firm.

For more than thirty-six years the Briggses owned part of the Tigers. Their influence stretched from 1920, when grandfather Walter O. Briggs became one of Frank Navin's silent partners, to 1956, when Briggs's trust was forced to sell the club. The park looks as it does today—with a double deck—because Briggs expanded it. When the renovation was done in 1938, he gave the field his name. His son Spike joined the organization in the mid-1930s. By the late 1940s Spike's three sons—Jim, Mickey, and Walter III—were inviting friends to play ball at their grandfather's park. In the 1950s they pitched batting practice to Al Kaline.

"What do you think about when you're here?" I ask Walter Briggs III.

I'm focused on taking notes, ready to write his response. When he doesn't answer, I figure he didn't hear the question. I glance up and he's staring out to right field, some family movie playing in his mind. His eyes have reddened and he swallows hard.

"My dad," he says.

At the end of the second inning, rain pours. During the delay, relief pitcher Todd Jones throws baseballs and packets of sunflower seeds to children. He works the crowd and they cheer. You get the sense that not only is he down-to-earth, but that he loves his job so much that he'll do whatever he can—even entertain during a rain delay—to add value to his role with the team. I am reminded what the official scorer, Chuck Klonke, told me days ago: "Todd Jones is a good guy, the kind you hope will do well."

As quickly as the storm comes, it disappears and the game resumes, and I find Carolyn Krause, who came from Boston to say farewell to Tiger Stadium, the sister park of her favorite, Fenway.

"Baseball has been the soundtrack to my life," she says. "I used to listen to games with my great-grandmother when she became too old to go. She lived to one hundred and four."

Her great-grandmother saw the first game at Fenway on April 20, 1912.

"That's the same day this park opened," I say, reciting a fact we both know. "They're the oldest parks in America."

"Actually," she says, "Fenway's an hour older. The game started earlier."

"Really?" I'm unconvinced.

Two seats in front of us, a Japanese doctor, Masatoshi Kondo, flinches when a three-inch plate from a rusted bolt falls from the catwalk above and hits his shoulder. "It's dangerous," he says. A stadium worker moves him to a better seat.

Krause attends about sixty-five games a year in Boston. She helps run Save Fenway Park!—an organization fighting efforts to replace the stadium with a modern replica.

"You can't fabricate history," she says. "When I want to see the Eiffel Tower, I don't go to Disney World; I go to Europe. As a country we should be embarrassed that we make everything disposable. I'm a Red Sox fan to my very core. But the Red Sox would not be the Red Sox without Fenway. The field is much bigger than any team."

Preservationists have never rescued an endangered park, I remind her. The efforts have failed at Comiskey, here, and elsewhere.

"Yes, there's never been a successful save," she says. "There's also never been a Fenway. Kevin Costner and W. P. Kinsella chose Fenway for a reason. Fenway means too much to so many people. Fenway and Wrigley are the two anomalies."

Deep inside, beyond the childhood insecurities that occasionally spring from my depths and cause me to get defensive, I know she must say that to give herself hope. I know she must believe it will be different for her park. Still, her words feel disrespectful, as if she's attacking the value of my memories and those of my father, my grandfather, and my sons, as if she's saying, *Well, it's unfortunate that your grandma died, but mine's more special anyway and maybe we can save her.*

Her words bother me because in part they are accurate. There is a perception that Fenway and Wrigley are more special than Tiger Stadium. I have struggled to understand it. Is it because those parks are in better neighborhoods? Or because their fans are more educated or affluent, more worldly? Or because they're based in Boston and Chicago, cities with grand literary traditions and writers who celebrate them? Or is it just because neither team has won a world championship since Hollywood began making talking movies and some find that romantic?

Our ballpark feels like Detroit. It carries no airs. It's blue-collar and industrial. When you enter through the gates, you come in beneath corrugated doors that have been rolled up on tracks, like at a warehouse delivery dock. You're greeted by cement and steel, strong, riveted girders that thrust upward and serve a purpose, holding the deck above in place. There are no architectural flourishes: no cornices, no fancy tile work, no aesthetic touches. This stadium shows its secrets—pipes, wires, girders, and all. It's plain and simple, no scent of pretentiousness. It doesn't yearn to be something it is not.

Krause may sense my irritation because her words take on a conciliatory tone.

"I feel like I couldn't help Tiger Stadium," she says. "But if Fenway can be preserved, at least part of that era can go on."

—— **Boston 11** ◇ **Detroit 4** ——

The Sox tag Jeff Weaver for nine runs in four innings, including a team-record five home runs.

**Game 55: Sunday, July 25** ◇ As "The Boys Are Back in Town" blasts from the speakers, the 1984 World Champion Tigers take the field for pre-game festivities.

There's fiery Jack Morris, a goatee looking especially trite on him. And Darrell Evans, the major-league veteran who became clubhouse leader. And reliever Guillermo Hernandez who, as Willie Hernandez, won the MVP and Cy Young awards. And Kirk Gibson, his clenched fists forever pumping skyward after his home run off Goose Gossage. And the others, too, on folding chairs in the infield, awash in the glow.

"Fifteen years later we meet back and salute the 1984 Detroit Tigers," says Ernie Harwell, and the crowd stands.

Detroit began that season 35–5 and never left first place. With 104 regular-season wins, Sparky Anderson's team was the most victorious in club history and it drew more people—2.7 million—than any other.

"I've been here many, many years," says Alan Trammell, addressing the fans, "but I don't know if I have had the chance to thank you. . . . It was a dream."

The current Tigers stare from the dugout, wondering what it would be like.

When columnist Joe Falls steps to the microphone, he gets polite applause mixed with boos. "We're losing our ballpark, and it's sad," he says. "But it's time."

Physically, I'm on the field with the working press; in spirit I'm in the stands with a smattering of others, jeering my former idol.

Who is he to tell us it's time?


—— **Detroit 9** ◇ **Boston 1** ——


Tony Clark hits two home runs. Dave Mlicki pitches a complete game.

The Stankiewiczes in 1983: Uncle Clem, Uncle Bucky,
Aunt Bernice, Uncle Ted, and Dad.

"I know they're in here," Uncle Teddy said. He
had plunged his left arm through an access panel between two
studs in an upstairs wall at the home on Montlieu. It was a Saturday in 1974 and I had pestered him into searching for baseball cards that, decades ago, he had stuffed into a hiding place.
"If I find them, you can have them."

"Did you have Babe Ruth?" I asked.

"Oh yeah." He glanced at my dad as if they would both
remember. "And Gehrig and Greenberg and Cochrane. All
them fellas."

Uncle Teddy had collected in the 1920s and 1930s, which
meant he had Goudey gum cards, maybe a 1933 of Ruth in

pinstripes against a lime background, or maybe some Delongs or Diamond Stars of Charlie Gehringer and Pie Traynor, or an American Caramel of Ty Cobb. With a little luck, maybe he had traded for some old cigarette cards and tucked a rare T-206 Honus Wagner, the world's most-desired baseball card, into the cigar box.

My own collection was limited to Topps gum cards bought at 7-Eleven: the blue-and-yellow–backed variety of 1970, with players' names in script on the front and each pack accompanied with a miniature comic booklet spotlighting men of such varied talents as Willie Mays, Cleon Jones, and Wally Bunker; and the black-bordered 1971 edition that looked so crisp when you got them but quickly advertised every scratch; and my favorites, the 1972 card with the boldly colored fronts in orange, green, and fuchsia and the gaudy marquee-type lettering and the special series of cards featuring players' boyhood photos that somehow reinforced just how likely it was that you would end up in the majors. There was Jim Fregosi with his accordion and Wilbur Wood with a fish he caught and Tom Seaver in a Little League uniform crouched on a ball field that could be anywhere, even Warren, Michigan. I sorted my cards by teams and kept them in rubber bands in empty Kodak boxes that Dad brought home from work. I treasured them, but what I really wanted were the cards I couldn't afford: the old ones featuring the men who had played at Navin Field, the cards that my uncle had long ago hid in the home on Montlieu.

Uncle Teddy had his entire arm inside the wall. He was standing on his toes, reaching down as far as he could so that the left side of his face—his shiny bald head, his ski-slope nose, his dimpled cheek—was pressed against the wall as if he were eavesdropping on the next room.

"I can't reach them," he said.

"Let's knock a hole in the wall," I suggested.

I was thirteen and he knew what baseball meant to me. I had told him what had happened days earlier. Three Detroit Tigers had moved into an apartment complex beyond the southern end zone of our Melby Junior High football field. This was unbelievable luck. Only once before had I seen a ballplayer outside the park, and that was at a benefit basketball game in a crowded gymnasium. Now John Hiller, Gary Sutherland, and Luke Walker were living in our neighborhood. Sutherland and Walker had come to Detroit in trades. They were journeymen with unspectacular careers. But John Hiller rated as a hero, a veteran of the 1968 championship team, who had recovered from a heart attack to become a star.

There are things I don't remember about the day I met Hiller—like who I was with. I do know it was a sunny summer morning, and there were three of us on bikes. One boy had a Schwinn Pea-Picker, with shock absorbers. And I heard Paul McCartney singing "Band on the Run"—or I imagine it, at least.

We were straddling our bikes in the parking lot wondering where, specifically, Hiller lived, when the American League's best relief pitcher pulled into the carport. He emerged in blue jeans and opened his trunk. Two of us hung back. The third spoke.

"Mr. Hiller, can we carry your groceries?"

He nodded. "Sure."

We ran to Hiller, who handed us each a bag.

In dazed silence we followed him across the asphalt onto the sidewalk to the front entrance of the eight-unit building, where he buzzed his apartment. The door buzzed back and we went up the carpeted stairs to the brown metal door on the left.

Hiller twisted the knob and we crossed the threshold, into his life. His wife and three children, one a baby, waited inside. She looked at us as if we were intruders. But I knew then we were destined to be much more. We were friends, not just fans. We were admirable young men who had gallantly spared a man with heart trouble the strain of taking his groceries up the stairs. I imagined this was only the start. He'd introduce his family. He'd offer us a soda, ask our names, shake our hands. I knew I'd help him again. I'd hang around the apartment and he'd get used to me, come to like me. That's how shy kids always picture it—that someone will see beyond their quiet to what no one else sees. Soon he'd invite me to the stadium, introduce me to Kaline and Horton, maybe hit me grounders at the Melby diamonds, show up at one of my games, and bestow upon me the status that comes to a boy whose close friend plays for the Tigers.

Of course, we never saw him again.

I had told Uncle Teddy all of this when it was still fresh in the mind, when we were in the house on Montlieu. And I'm sure he could relate. I'm sure he could imagine himself at Gehringer's home and what that would have meant.

Regardless, he wasn't about to punch through the upstairs wall. He had lived on Montlieu since before the Depression. After the war he and Aunt Sadie moved into the upstairs, which he and his pa had converted into an apartment. His parents lived below. Eventually, after his parents died, Uncle Teddy bought the house from his siblings. He lived in it longer than anyone. When the neighborhood became infested with crime in the 1970s, he installed bars on the windows and kept the back door barricaded with a plank, the kind used in TV westerns. On our visits Dad never allowed me in the alley behind the scraggly remnants of Pa's rosebushes. "It's not safe," he said.

But it was safe enough for elderly women like Mrs. Konczal, who still lived there and sat on her porch and waved to Dad as he drove past, recognizing him from those many years ago when he and her son played for the Crusaders.

The burglaries that plagued the area had prompted Uncle Teddy to consider selling the home, though he knew he wouldn't get much for it.

"The cards are worth more than the house," I said.

Those words—compelling evidence to a child—must have burned him, for he pulled his arm from the wall and announced that the cards weren't there. And that was that.

As we were about to leave, Aunt Sadie nudged my stubborn uncle and whispered as she always did, "Give him something." They both worked, had no children, and were generous with nephews and nieces. Uncle Teddy pressed a folded $20 bill into my palm and gave me his dumb, dimpled grin.

What I really wanted was in the wall.

◇ ◇ ◇ ◇ ◇ ◇ ◇  *The Fist*

**Game 56: Monday, August 2** ◇ The Tigers return home after a six-game losing streak, as hopeful as a Texas death-row inmate. Bobby Higginson is injured, pitcher Bryce Florie has been sent to Boston, and the team could claim baseball's worst record.

"I'm counting the days," says Al the Usher.

Every fan recalls a torturous season: 1996; 1989; 1975; 1952. Those Detroit teams lost more than a hundred games. When you're a kid whose life revolves around baseball, it matters.

Kevin Brender was such a boy, dark-haired and slender, the kind who stood off in the corner at family weddings with a transistor radio to his ear, listening to Ernie Harwell. From

1971 through 1975, he spent a good sixteen hundred hours consuming games. That figures out to be sixty-five days straight, twenty-four hours a day.

"It cost me a fortune in nine-volt batteries," he says.

Brender would station himself at the kitchen table of his *Wonder Years* home, biting his nails and recalculating Mickey Lolich's earned-run average after each inning, multiplying earned runs by nine and dividing the sum by innings pitched, taking care not to count runs scored on errors—doing it with a diligence few applied to homework, doing it as if the world hung on the fact that Lolich had lowered that number by one-hundredth of a point.

"Oh yeah, I was sick," he says now, at age thirty-seven a partner in a major accounting firm. "In 1975 when they lost 102 ball games, I listened to every game during the nineteen-game losing streak. It killed me. When the Tigers lost, I would be depressed the next day."

There is joy in connecting with a fan your age who not only shares the obsession, but shared it at the same time and for the same team. You needn't explain why you hated Bert Campaneris (for throwing a bat at Lerrin LaGrow). Or why the Nate Colbert trade filled you with hope in 1974 (because it meant Willie Horton would have a power hitter behind him). Or why you know Cesar Gutierrez's name (seven consecutive hits in one game). It must be the same feeling an Elvis impersonator gets when he spots the familiar black sideburns.

If Brender and I had grown up in the same neighborhood, we would have been buddies.

It's not a casual fan, after all, who does what Brender did on July 13, 1985. The Tigers were on the road and the ballpark was empty. Brender parked his car near the ticket booth at Michigan and Trumbull. "The place was like a ghost town," he says. His girlfriend, Kris Binsfeld, was in the passenger's seat.

"What are we doing here?" she asked.

"I want to propose to you," he said.

She was surprised by the setting, not the question.

"It was no more than three or four minutes," he says. "We got back in the car and drove over to Canada for pizza. To this day I think she regrets the way I did it. I don't know what possessed me to do it here."

I do.

—— **Chicago 6** ◇ **Detroit 2** ——

Sox rookie Kip Wells wins his major-league debut.

**Game 57: Tuesday, August 3** ◇ I saw an old *Andy Griffith Show* episode the other day. A spoilt child had moved to town and was teaching "Opie" to throw tantrums. The kid convinced Opie that his pa was being unfair by paying 25 cents allowance and requiring Opie to complete a list of chores. Opie experimented with tears and foot-stomping; neither worked. Sheriff Andy was too good a father to be drawn into that. He remained calm but stern. Eventually the new kid got spanked behind the police shed, his lenient father seeing the error in his permissiveness. By show's end the whole sordid affair was over. Andy's unwavering wisdom had prevailed, and Opie was back to being Opie and on his way to becoming Richie Cunningham.

Tonight Mayberry is a world away.

A few hours ago I had an argument with my teenage son. Zack announced that he wasn't going on a long-planned family trip to an Ohio amusement park.

"Why not?"

"I don't want to."

The dispute escalated quickly, each of us growing more stubborn.

"You're going," I said. "We already bought the tickets."

My younger sons watched the words whip out of control. Soon I had raised the price for Zack's defiance. "Then you're going to have pay for the ticket," I yelled. "And there will be no TV for a week."

"Fine!" he said, stomping up to his room.

I left for the ballpark, crushed, a failure as a father.

Now, alone in the stands, I am removed from the frivolity on the field. The players take batting practice and coach Lance Parrish shakes hands with second baseman Damion Easley, whose wife gave birth to another son. Even the manager can smile, and he has lost seven straight.

Me? I feel like a fist.

I love so much about my son. He's unusual for a fourteen-year-old; he relishes partisan politics and Otis Redding songs, knows the words to every Allan Sherman parody, and listens to CDs of great American speeches. "He was born an old man," my wife has joked.

Recently Zack confessed that he had borrowed $20 three years ago and we never asked him to repay it. "It's been bothering me," he said, handing us the money.

We were at band camp last week. I chaperoned and Zack did everything he could to avoid me. We exchanged maybe ten words.

"It'll get better," one mother said. "Wait until he's a senior."

I've enjoyed seeing Zack grow from the little boy I once pushed on our tree swing, into the young man who has a deep voice, soft whiskers, and eyes that sigh at female figures. He makes me feel proud; I wish I made him feel that way.

—— **Chicago 9** ◇ **Detroit 6** ——

Dean Palmer sets a Tiger record for third basemen when he hits his twenty-sixth home run. The team loses its eighth consecutive game. Afterward, Palmer talks about the team's failure to live up to expectations. "It's tough to accept the fact you're bad," he says.

**Game 58: Friday, August 13** ◇ Two storms have come and gone on this humid day and the pigeons are flitting in and out of the stands. Twenty-four games remain—6,849 have been played. "I try not to think about it," says Mary Pletta, who has been serving hot dogs and pop for twenty-one seasons. "The years just keep folding away on me."

I brought my camera today, a Canon AE1. I'm taking pictures to ensure that after my memory is gone I will have something to show for this season in the stands. I shoot the seats, the fence, the field. I shoot the dugouts and bullpens. I shoot the ramps that hug the contours of the park and connect the decks, but the lighting is spotty. The other day, as Dad and I ambled down a ramp, he flashed back to a visit with his own father. He remembered running so fast on the incline that his legs felt as if they wouldn't keep up with his body. His pa warned him to slow down if he didn't want to fall on the concrete and knock out his teeth.

In the press box upstairs tonight, I hear a visiting reporter ask a local writer, "You glad to see this place go?"

"Well, there are memories," the Detroiter says. "But once the fans see the new place, they'll forget all about this one."

## ———— Detroit 8 ◇ Anaheim 7 ————

Tony Clark ties the game with a home run, sending it into extra innings. In the tenth Dean Palmer singles in Brad Ausmus.

**Game 59: Saturday, August 14** ◇ After months of encouragement from parking-lot owner Howard Stone—"You gotta talk to Baker"—I finally corner Thaddeus Baker, a wide man in a white designer sweatsuit. Baker sells brown bags of hand-packed peanuts at a card table along Stone's lot. He's been doing it since 1964. "When we won the pennant in '68, it was money back then," he says. "Kaline, Horton—there was money down here."

Sidewalk vendors come early to secure their spots. They dot the dirt-and-cement landscape around Cochrane Avenue. Baker always gets his place. He has the seniority, and having given so many others in the area their break, he commands respect on the street. He has the kind of standing that allows him to walk into any game free of charge.

"Everybody's out of business after this season," says Baker who, according to Howard, has a gun strapped to his leg. "We can't vendor in the downtown area [near the new park]. This is it. We got twenty-three games left. After that it's over with. I think it's wrong. Some of these people down here need the income."

A retired school worker with a decent pension, Baker doesn't rely on the money. He says he enjoys the bustle outside the park and gets satisfaction putting local kids to work. He pays a quarter for each bag they sell. "As it goes down to the wire, it gets rough," he says. "Everybody's selling stuff cheaper to get rid of it." Baker's peanuts go two bags for a buck.

Inside the park Al the Usher has his own challenges. Yesterday he caught a guy snipping a section of fencing as a souvenir. "What the hell are you doing?" said Al, confronting a man fifty years younger. Al expects to spend his final weeks at the stadium "watching the donkeys tear it apart."

Today more than 35,000 have turned out on a breezy afternoon. The crowds have begun to increase and it's not because of the baseball, which has been dismal. They're coming to see the stadium—fathers and sons and grandfathers with cameras in hand—and they're buying lots of Art Witkosky's hot dogs and Amzie Griffin's *Baseball at The Corner* T-shirts.

In the center-field bleachers, Pete Munoz, with little angels pinned to his Anaheim ball cap, has competition for his preferred seat, a few rows up from where Ken Griffey made that catch last year. After the sixth inning, after Tony Clark's home run, he begins telling me again about Griffey, the photo in the magazine, and the elusive autograph.

"Did you get a ticket yet for the last game?" I ask.

"Nope. I'll get one next week," he says.

I hope he does, but my mind is already on tomorrow and Uncle Tom. That's the day he and Dad get together. I've tried to picture how it might go. It's tough to know. Dad has said he won't be surprised if his brother cancels at the last minute. But I know my dad. He's simply guarding against overenthusiasm.

—— **Anaheim 7** ◇ **Detroit 4** ——

Gabe Kapler, the rookie who showed so much promise early in the season, is struggling: one hit in twenty-nine at-bats. Contrary to rumors, team president John McHale says he expects manager Larry Parrish to be back next year.

Dad and Uncle Tom.

**Game 60: Sunday, August 15** ◇ "Did you hear Pee Wee Reese died?"

This is my uncle Tom talking and he's looking right at my dad, his older brother Joe. This makes the third time they've seen each other in the past twenty-seven years. You wouldn't guess it, though. They talk as if they'd never lost touch.

About Pee Wee Reese: Dad doesn't hear Uncle Tom's words but he tries to bluff it, as he always does. If it's just a statement—not a question—he'll smile his way through, nodding for emphasis, and you'll presume he heard you. He keeps the conversation moving that way, picking up bits and pieces, getting a general sense of it.

"Did you hear Pee Wee Reese died?" Uncle Tom says louder.

Dad still doesn't get it.

"Pee Wee Reese! Brooklyn Dodgers!"

"Oh yeah. I thought you said did I see 'TV's Reese fly.' Pee Wee Reese. He was a good one."

Fourteen years separate them. Dad was the fifth child; Uncle Tom the youngest of ten. "A lot of your growing up, I was either in service or married," says Dad. "I wasn't around."

"I felt like an only child between the age difference and the war years," says Uncle Tom. "Times were different when I was growing up. Baseball was everything. There was no TV. Not many cars. A war was going on. Every Sunday Pa would go to either Belle Isle or Northwestern Field. We would go to five-thirty mass, come home, eat breakfast, pack a lunch, and go to the ball game. He'd buy a pop for me and a pop for him and two cigars. Ten o'clock, we'd watch the industrial league. One o'clock, we'd watch the younger kids play. Three o'clock, he had a nephew that played and we'd go to see them games."

It was a story I had heard many times, only the names changed. Sometimes it was Dad. Sometimes Clem or Bucky or Teddy. Grandpa liked to spend marathon Sundays watching amateurs play.

"I tried to con Pa into taking me to a Tiger game," says Uncle Tom. "His answer all the time was, if the game wasn't any good he had to sit through it because he had paid sixty cents. If we went to the other ballpark and he didn't like it, he'd walk to the next diamond to find a game. There were like ten diamonds and he'd find a good game."

My dad listens and nods.

"The first time I went to a Tiger baseball game was in '46," Uncle Tom continues. "I was twelve. Clem conned Ted and Herb into forking over money to Pa to take me to a game. We went to a twilight game. It started at five-thirty or six-thirty. It was Briggs Stadium. Pa called it Navin Field. Roy Cullenbine hit two home runs and Greenberg hit a three-bagger to the flagpole. Virgil Trucks was pitching. He hit a ball the same place and ended up with a double."

"Newhouser was here then," Dad says.

"Yeah, TNT: Trucks, Newhouser, and Trout. Remember that?"

"Yep, Virgil Trucks."

Despite the years of difference they look like brothers, both in ball caps with big eyeglasses, and the rounded bellies that join us Stankiewiczes in middle age and never depart. Occasionally they break from conversation to watch the game, which the Tigers are losing. Gabe Kapler is again wearing his pants so his socks show.

As much as I enjoy their exchanges, I find what they don't say just as telling. *Where have you been all these years? Why didn't you call? What happened? Did I do something to hurt you? Why this long?* Perhaps neither raises these questions out of fear, for finally they are with one another. Would the answers really be worth the risk of insult or injury? After all this time it could balance precariously on a sharp inflection. They've missed enough already. Uncle Tom missed the funerals of two brothers. Dad missed the weddings of his nephews and niece. For most of three decades they've been absent from each other's lives.

Over the years family members would report that they had seen someone who might be Uncle Tom from across a parking lot or at a department store. No one was ever certain, and at this moment in this ballpark it matters to neither of them.

"When I was a kid, Pa always had the game on the radio," says Uncle Tom. "I remember he used to love Tommy Bridges because Tommy Bridges was about five foot tall. Pa was not very tall. He looked up to Tommy Bridges. He would brag about his curveball. He was small and yet he could strike out these big hitters."

"I used to get a kick out of Pa watching the ball game," says Dad. "He'd be moving his feet. If the guy was sliding, he'd be throwing his feet out. He'd do the actions."

"Well," adds Uncle Tom, "you should have seen him watch a wrasslin' match. Holy cripe! He believed in that and he believed in cowboy movies. When a guy got shot, he really thought he got shot. It was funny."

They reminisce about a Pinky Higgins baseball glove, Pa's roses, the *Polish Daily News*, Holy Name School, and their brothers, including Herb, whom I have not yet located.

I have scant childhood memories of Herb and Tom. Actually, I'm not sure they're even memories. It may be that I've convinced myself that I remember the scenes pictured in photo albums. There's Tom's wedding, with me, four years old, in a tux. There's one of Herb in his Air Force uniform, a staid pose in the corner of our living room. There's another of me in Grandma's heavy, sagging arms, with Tom, a college student, beside her.

"When I went with Pa, we'd be underneath that dang scoreboard," my uncle says, nodding toward the bleachers. "I was scared of heights. He liked the shade. He thought he got a better view of the field. Sitting up there and looking down that incline scared the heck out of me. He was a baseball fan; he wasn't always a Tiger fan. He'd go to cheer Ted Williams or Johnny Pesky or Dominic DiMaggio. He said, 'I cheer for the best team.' I remember Connie Mack being here, Hank Majeski, Kell. Barney McCosky was one of Pa's favorites. They traded him for George Kell."

"McCosky. He had the right name," says Dad.

"When we made that trade, to Pa it was almost like the Kuenn and Colavito trade. I know people at work when Kuenn got traded, they wouldn't come to another Tiger ball game. I liked Kuenn a lot, though Colavito ended up being a better player for longer. Pa liked Ted Williams, Joe DiMaggio, Greenberg. Tommy Bridges was his number one. He used to talk about Elden Auker, too."

Uncle Tom bites into his turkey-and-mustard sandwich, a concession to his high blood pressure and heart problems. "It's probably my imagination but food tasted better then," he says. "I'm trying to remember how my stomach ever survived eating kishka. Ma would buy this kishka and fry it with grease. The grease was dripping off this stuff."

"You could hear it popping," says Dad.

"This was for breakfast and then we'd pour ketchup on it. Holy cripe!"

"It tasted pretty good."

"I know it did. They'd pile it on your plate. It's chunks of liver, barley, and blood, I think."

There's a pause in the conversation as if Dad's reflecting on being in the ballpark with his brother all these many years later.

"I like this," he says.

"Me too," says Uncle Tom.

—— **Anaheim 7** ◇ **Detroit 2** ——

◇ ◇ ◇ ◇ ◇ ◇ ◇   *Red Dust*

**Game 61: Monday, August 16** ◇ In 1973 Ed Stych came to Tiger Stadium for the first time with his parents and younger brother. They made the cross-state trip and sat by the visitors' bullpen where Ed got Rollie Fingers's and Darold Knowles's autographs.

"I clearly remember wishing that we were closer to home plate but thankful nonetheless that my parents drove us all the way from Traverse City," he says. "Between nine and eighteen I pretty much lived and breathed baseball. I didn't get down here to see many games, so it was special when I did. This was our cathedral."

Now living in Minneapolis where he owns three print shops, Stych wanted to share the park of his youth with his oldest son, nine-year-old Joey. "I've had this trip planned for a couple of years," he says.

He wants to tell Joey about Kaline and about Gibson's home run in the 1984 Series, a feat witnessed by Ed and his wife Anne. He wants to point to the light standard where Reggie Jackson deposited his All-Star game round-tripper and to the radio booth from which Ernie Harwell bridged the distance of 242 miles.

Tonight by coincidence they have nearly the same seats as Ed had in 1973, right by the bullpen. "It provides some nice symmetry to my personal history here," he says.

After the game, under a Van Gogh sky, Ed walks the field with his son as part of a run-the-bases promotion. Behind home plate atop the park glow the blue neon letters that face Michigan Avenue and proclaim this Tiger Stadium. As the Styches exit the field, Joey reaches over and drags three fingers on the warning track. For the next hour he's careful not to rub the red dust from his hand.

Ed has paintings of Tiger Stadium, of his and Anne's childhood homes, of the first house they owned together, and of the building where their church group meets. "I'm not sure why these structures mean so much to me," he says. "I guess they are reminders of memories of important times in my life.

"To me there's a spirituality to baseball," he says. "In football if you're down by three touchdowns and you're running out of time, you know you're going to lose. In baseball you sit there listening to Harwell. The Tigers are down by five. But they still have a chance. There is no clock and there's always an opportunity for redemption."

—— **Tampa Bay 9** ◇ **Detroit 1** ——

Jeff Weaver gets hit hard, giving up seven runs in four innings.

**Game 62: Tuesday, August 17** ◇ Kirk Gibson, the outspoken former Tiger, criticized Tampa Bay's Wade Boggs days ago because Boggs had kissed home plate after collecting his three-thousandth hit. Gibson, who made it halfway to that plateau, said that such flamboyant gestures have kept Boggs from earning respect. Boggs, forty-one, heard about Gibson's comments and responded. Today both men are on the field before the game.

As Gibson heads into the dugout, Boggs calls out, "Hey, Kirk." They meet along the third-base line and Gibson does most of the talking for ten minutes. There is no yelling or smiling, just words delivered calmly. They part with a stiff handshake.

Behind the batting cage Al Kaline congratulates the future Hall of Famer, who is four hits shy of Kaline's 3,007. Gabe Kapler also offers his hand.

Yesterday Boggs said he'd like to surpass Kaline in this park.

"I think it would be memorable if nothing else to do it in Tiger Stadium. I like hitting here," he said. "It is one of the better parks I've had success in. But I think it's time for a new one, with the small dugouts and the small clubhouse. Nowadays players like the comfort of larger atmospheres."

During batting practice the scoreboard runs footage of Boggs and Tony Gwynn reaching their milestones. Boggs watches as his dad appears. Afterward, he practices his swing and proceeds to the cage where he slaps a few balls into the outfield.

—— **Detroit 3** ◇ **Tampa Bay 1** ——

Dave Mlicki, the only bright spot among the starters, wins his third straight, allowing five hits in seven innings.

**Game 63: Wednesday, August 18** ◇ If you pick at the chipped paint in the Tiger dugout, you can get beyond the glossy blue to the rough concrete and the pebbles embedded in it. The paint is so heavy that it snaps when it breaks. If it cracks just right, you can see a coat of green beneath the blue. Before the late 1970s, the dugout, like the rest of the stadium interior, was park-bench green.

The roof, eight inches thick, looks as if it is coated in percolating lava and it feels like glass, like glazed pottery, but rippled with the roughness and imperfections that testify to its age. Two cement columns, also blue, brace the roof, on which the mascot Paws occasionally dances.

Everyone who visits the field tries to make it into the dugout. Out-of-town writers, celebrity guests—they all yearn to take the three steps down toward the hallowed bench, possibly the smallest in the majors. And it's accepted behavior, so accepted that a sign on the wall sets the limits: *This dugout will be closed to all media members and other non-uniformed personnel forty minutes before game time—Detroit Baseball Club.* The dugout measures twenty-five feet or so and lacks enough bench space for the whole team. During the game some sit on the steps or on a stool outside, visible to fans. It's where Bobby Higginson prefers to watch, facing the plate.

On the cushioned bench leaning against the slatted back, your feet resting on a plank scratched bare of paint, you find your eyes at the level of the raised pitcher's mound. No view from the home bench along third base encompasses the entire field. To see a ball hit down the line in left, you would have to move. It's a familiar scene when a right-hander pulls one high and deep. The ball draws the players up toward the field.

To your left is the dark, cavelike tunnel that connects the clubhouse. First baseman Tony Clark, six feet seven inches, must walk hunched through it. Men were shorter when it was built. To your right is a rack for bats. They are displayed so players' uniform numbers show on the knobs. Before the contest a batboy sits in front of the rack near sweating pipes, rubbing muddy water into game balls to improve their feel and reduce their glare.

A few things betray the dugout's age: the bullpen phone, the plastic coolers, and the wires that snake along the walls. Otherwise it is old and authentic and awe-inspiring. For most of my life this has been a secretive, mysterious place, off-limits except in my dreams.

This is as close as you can get to Cobb, Heilmann, and manager Hughie Jennings, who motivated runners by stomping his knee and yelling, "Eeh-jah," as they raced toward home. This is where Charlie Gehringer silently went about his business and where Hank Greenberg, the first Jewish star, perched on the step before grabbing his bat, ascending to the on-deck circle, and filling a thousand boys with anticipation. Baseball history books are loaded with photos taken on the edge of this dugout: Ruth shaking hands with Mickey Cochrane and Frankie Frisch before the '34 Series; Bridges, Newsom, and Schoolboy posing in 1940; a young Al Kaline meeting Ted Williams. It is from this dugout that Willie Horton barreled onto the field when fights erupted and from here that Mark "The Bird" Fidrych emerged to tip his cap as fans chanted for him and from which Sparky leapt when his team won in 1984. It is here as a boy that I, like a million other kids—like my father and his brothers thirty and forty years earlier— dreamed of being someday, in uniform, in the lineup, on the team. For most of us visitors to the field, sitting on the bench before the game is as close as we'll come.

Today Michael Litaker and Wes Easley are in the dugout.

"If World War Three breaks out, I want to be in here," says Litaker. "This is a bomb shelter."

Litaker, a camera in his hand, shoots photos for the Topps baseball-card company. Easley, a groundskeeper, works every game and most of the time I can find him in here a few minutes before batting practice finishes and he springs back into action.

"At the end of the game you see people pointing and telling their stories," he says. "In April people asked me how it feels, this being the last season. I said, 'Ask me in September.' I'm feeling it now. Eighteen more games. It's starting to hit me."

—— **Tampa Bay 4** ◇ **Detroit** ○ ——

Gabe Kapler, with his pant legs pulled over his socks, gets a triple, the team's only hit.

◇ ◇ ◇ ◇ ◇ ◇ ◇   *Dr. Livingood's Flag*

Cal Ripken Jr.

**Game 64: Friday, August 27** ◇ The public countdown has started. "Monthlong Wake Begins..." proclaims the lead headline in today's *Detroit News*. A white sign, with a big red 18, hangs in the third deck. After the fifth inning when the game becomes official, Aaron Copeland's regal "Fanfare for the Common Man" plays and the card is removed, revealing a 17; and tomorrow a 16; and so on, until no games remain.

It's been four months since I embarked on this mission and in that time I've heard this place described affectionately by hundreds of fans. Some call it Tiger Stadium; others, Briggs Stadium or Navin Field, names engraved upon their memories in youth. To many it's simply The Corner—Michigan and Trumbull. When Al Kaline came, he saw a battleship; Lance Parrish, a warehouse; sportswriter Joe Falls, a barn. Don Hall, the poet, compared it to a frail grocer "who wears a straw hat and a blue necktie." Like all revered ballparks, it is a shrine, a field of dreams, a green cathedral. To those inclined to ascribe gender, the park is a woman: Grand Lady, Queen of Diamonds. To Steve Olsen, the scorekeeper, it is simply "old friend." To Pete Munoz in the bleachers, "my home."

I went to Wrigley Field twice, once in winter and once in summer when it rained. Other than those visits, I've never been to another major-league park. I've not witnessed a game outside of Tiger Stadium. Of course, I've gotten glimpses of other parks on television. But you know it's not the same.

It's only in Tiger Stadium from the outfield stands that I've heard ball hit bat just after seeing it, like bad lip-synching in a foreign film. It's only here that I've felt the bleachers shake during a foot-stomping rally and smelt the blend of cigars and sausage and held my dad's hand as a boy and braced his arm as a man.

For me Tiger Stadium is the keeper of a million memories.

—— **Detroit 5** ◇ **Baltimore 4** ——

Jeff Weaver rekindles the early-season optimism, allowing four hits in eight innings and getting the win after Damion Easley and Gabe Kapler homer.

**Game 65: Saturday, August 28** ◇ Sixteen years ago, one question separated Todd Miller from lunch with Ernie Harwell.

"Who's Mayo Smith?"

Miller answered correctly and got to eat with Harwell and members of the Mayo Smith Society, a club named for the 1968 manager. It was no small prize.

Raised in Michigan, Miller became a Tiger fan despite his father, an Ann Arbor dentist who maintained a boyhood allegiance to Boston. In 1967 the American League pennant came down to the last day of the season. A win in the second game of a doubleheader would have forced a one-game playoff between the Tigers and Sox. But the Tigers lost and a heartbroken Todd Miller watched his dad celebrate.

"Ernie Harwell was my link to the Tigers when I was growing up," says Miller. "He has such a congenial way of talking that you can't help but like everything he says. He is the reason I'm a Tiger fan. Because of Ernie Harwell I've kept my loyalty."

A marketing consultant, Miller lives in Pittsburgh and tunes in to Harwell. Occasionally he makes it back home. This weekend he and sons Ross and Evan came for the Mayo Smith Society's annual gathering, a celebration made more special by the July appointment of Dale Petroskey, a society founder, as president of the National Baseball Hall of Fame.

Miller says, "I consider Tiger Stadium a refuge where you can forget about the day and you can think of the game and all the great players—Ty Cobb and Babe Ruth and contemporary stars, Ken Griffey Jr. and Cal Ripken Jr. The new parks all have outfields that show the downtown skylines. I like being able to forget about the problems outside. I like it when there's nothing in front of me except the ball game."

The Tigers look like a playoff team today. In the third inning Gabe Kapler leads off with a triple to left-center. Deivi Cruz doubles him home. Kimera Bartee moves him to third on a bunt and Brad Ausmus squeezes in Cruz.

Baseball is pretty when played well.

—— **Detroit 4** ◇ **Baltimore 3** ——

Dave Mlicki wins his fifth straight, raising his record to 10–10, best on the team.

**Game 66: Sunday, August 29** ◇ Among an acre of empty seats, the Reverend Jeff Totten, a confident man with a brush cut, studies the sermon he will deliver around noon in the locker room. Totten, the Tigers' pastor, represents Baseball Chapel, an organization that encourages Christian players to live their faith. He preaches before every Sunday home game and travels to meet players on the road. Ernie Harwell introduced us early in the season.

In the majors there is a thriving brotherhood of athletes who have publicly proclaimed their devotion to Christ. Among them are current and former Tigers Damion Easley, Todd Jones, Lance Parrish, Travis Fryman, and Frank Tanana, a 240-game winner who found God after the death of a friend and a career-threatening injury.

Totten looks up as I approach, eager to tell me about Cal Ripken Jr.

"Yesterday I brought my son and two of his Little League buddies down," he says. "They got in early, sat right by the dugout, each with a ball and with one purpose, to get Ripken's autograph. Of course Ripken, after he did his workout, started signing at this end and worked his way to the dugout. He got down to their end right near game time. He signed one kid's ball, signed my son's ball, and signed the ball of my son's other buddy."

Ripken smudged the last signature but no one complained.

"I'm sorry," Ripken said. "I messed up. That's not too neat.

Let me get you another one." Ripken continued along the dugout for ten minutes, rewarding more fans.

"Sure enough," says Totten, "he went in, got a fresh ball, ran it out, and resigned it. I never heard of a player doing that."

The Orioles have visited the park twice this season. Both times Ripken has been unable to play. It's been a rough year for him, between his own injuries and the death of his father, Cal Ripken Sr. But he knows that many come to see him. So he takes batting practice, swinging tenderly to avoid pain, mostly looping soft hits into the outfield. And they cheer.

When Lou Gehrig came to Detroit in May 1939 and decided not to play in his 2,131st straight game, he delivered the lineup card to the umpire at home plate and Briggs Stadium erupted in a loud, prolonged ovation.

"I was just a little shit," Irv Marshall, seventy-three, said earlier in Howard Stone's parking lot. "My aunt took me to that ball game. I said to her, 'Hey, they just announced the lineup and Gehrig's name isn't in there.' I used to follow the Yankees like so many people did. And damn if he did not play that day. It was *buzz, buzz, buzz.*"

This afternoon, with a cloud shadow sweeping across the field, Ripken carries the lineup card to the plate, where he meets Alan Trammell and the umpires. Those who notice stand and applaud. It is their thank-you and they might remember this moment until they die, for Ripken won't be back.

The stories of this ballpark—from Gehrig's last visit to Reggie's All-Star home run—are the stories of shared experiences, each witnessed by tens of thousands and retold by more, embedded not only in the lives of individuals but in the life of a community. I've listened to dozens of fans recall the 1984 World Series. Almost all have mentioned Gibson's heroics, the home run off Gossage in the final game. But the textures differ—the specifics—where they sat, bleachers or box, and whether they brought a high-school buddy, a brother, or a fiancée, and what it felt like through their eyes—some experiencing it for the first time, some relating it to 1935 and Mickey Cochrane and Goose Goslin and their long-dead grandfather in his straw cap and dark suspenders. Still, there is a common thread.

John Pilarowski felt it in the 1968 Series. He had gotten married October 5 of that year and spent the next day, his honeymoon, at the park with his wife Jenny, snuggling in the rain as the Cardinals pummeled the Tigers. John and Jenny had met that spring and seen, together or apart, thirty games.

"Every game it was a different hero," he says, sitting beside Jenny in the upper deck. "Blacks and whites. Earl Wilson, Horton, Kaline, Jim Northrup, Gates Brown. I saw McLain win his thirtieth and thirty-first."

A year earlier, in 1967, race riots had claimed forty-three lives in Detroit. Pilarowski had worked downtown with the United States Health Service, two blocks from the turmoil. "It looked like World War Two," he remembers. "There were convoys with jeeps. Barbed wire. Soldiers with guns. Machine-gun fire popping off bricks and *Soul Brother* painted on buildings. Nineteen sixty-eight put the city back together. The people came out on the streets. The people in the suburbs came back downtown."

No one who lived through it could ever doubt that what happened in that ballpark that championship summer meant something more than a game should.

—— **Baltimore 11** ◇ **Detroit 4** ——

Damion Easley gets two homers. He has four in the last three games.

**Game 67: Monday, August 30** ◇ I pull into Howard Stone's lot and he hits me with a question. "Did you hear? . . . Baker died." Thaddeus Baker, the king of the street peanut salesmen, passed away Sunday at age fifty-nine. Already another vendor has grabbed his corner.

"He trained that guy," says John, Howard's son-in-law. "He showed him where to buy the peanuts and everything. A couple months ago he opened up shop across the street up a corner to beat out Baker. Baker's own brother did that to him last year."

"He was a good man," says Irv Marshall. "I remember he was working over here, where the table is, and some guy's giving him a bad time—a young kid, maybe in his early twenties. He says, 'Hey old man, get out of my face before I rip you apart.' And Baker says, 'What?'—and he's looking up at the guy. The next thing—*bang*!—and it was over. The kid was knocked out on the sidewalk. Then Baker says, 'The next time, I'm gonna shoot you.' "

"If Baker showed up today," notes Howard, nodding at the corner, "that guy would move."


In 1916 Francis Geck went to his first ball game at Navin Field with his German grandfather. Today, eighty-three years later, he came back in a wheelchair he says he doesn't need. He was a boy of fifteen then; a man of ninety-eight now. He hasn't seen any games in the years between.

"That is a long span. Eighty-some years. That is a long time," Geck says. "This sort of gives me a chill." For most of those decades he lived in New York, Paris, and Boulder, Colorado, a professor of interior design. In Detroit he worked on the elaborate, wood-paneled executive offices that once graced Albert Kahn's Fisher Building.

Geck has forgotten details of the 1916 visit. "Everything is vague to me," he says. "It was just a little sort of amateur park at that time. For some reason my grandfather thought I ought to see Ty Cobb play. Of course, as I say, my grandfather lived just across the street over there."

He points toward Trumbull Avenue, where his family owned several homes. "I played football and tennis but never baseball," he says. "I was never able to catch a ball nor was I ever able to bat a ball."

Geck reaches into his shirt pocket, retrieves a piece of paper, and unfolds it. "I composed a little ditty," he says. He asks me to read it.

" 'It is to become a playtime where batters, pitchers, wait, perchance to become . . . ' "

I could spend the whole game with Francis Geck and enjoy every minute of it. Instead I leave that pleasure to his family and friends and return to my father in section 217.

"Sorry, Dad. I didn't mean to abandon you here."

"No, you do what you have to do," he says. "I'm fine."

"Are you getting tired of coming to the games yet?"

"No," he says. "I know you like them."

All season the Tigers have been flying a reminder of my dad's mortality. On the flagpole in center field beneath the Stars and Stripes is a simple tribute with the initials *CSL*, honoring Clarence Livingood, the team physician who died in the off-season.

"I don't think I ever told you this before," Dad says. "When you were little, I thought I was dying. I had a growth near my spine and I went to a doctor. He called me at work and said, 'You have cancer.' I thought I was going to die. I didn't tell nobody, even your mom. I didn't want to worry all of you. It scared the hell out of me."

A friend at work recommended he see another doctor.

"Dr. Livingood looked at it and said, 'You're going to be fine.' The other guy was a quack, put me through all that worry for nothing. Dr. Livingood cut it off and I never had another problem with it."

Hearing about this awakens old anxieties.

For all my dad's numerous annoyances—the way he jangled his coins, the way he dredged his throat clear, the way he'd lay his arm over my shoulder in public, without warning—I loved him dearly. I loved him in the distant, unspoken, "don't force me to admit it" way that fifteen-year-old boys love their fathers.

Dad was fifty-six when I was fifteen and I feared he might die. Perhaps it grew out of Mom's bout with brain tumors and how they had entered our life suddenly and changed her permanently, paralyzing her right side. Maybe it was because he was the oldest dad on our street. Every day I scanned the obituary page of the *Macomb Daily*, checking the ages of the deceased. Lots of men died in their fifties. Heart attacks and cancer, I guessed. Both ran in our family.

Grandma Muse, my mom's mother, died that summer. She had lived a full life, they said. At school that year, two brothers became orphaned after a car accident, and down the street Joe Koslakiewicz, a ball-playing buddy, lost his father. He had collapsed on the kitchen floor, his physical presence forever removed from his son's life.

It seemed the cruelest of fates.

That summer Dad and I went to several ball games. The Tigers had traded Mickey Lolich for Rusty Staub and we liked to watch the red-haired right fielder. We admired Ron LeFlore's speed and Jason Thompson's power, and he'd tell me about Pinky Higgins and Charlie Maxwell, who hit home runs on Sundays. Whatever else was happening in our lives, we still had baseball and I still had my dad.

—— **Detroit** 1 ◇ **Texas** 0 ——

Brian Moehler three-hits the first-place Rangers. Gabe Kapler homers in the seventh. Earlier in the day, Moehler and Kapler went with their wives to Lamaze breathing classes.

**Game 68: Tuesday, August 31** ◇ I like to sit in the covered lower bleachers in right-center on the highest bench which, unlike the rest out here, was never replaced with ridged metal. It's wood. Save for a few splatters, the blue paint has worn off and the original green shows through, along with seat numbers stenciled in yellow.

My grandpa liked to sit in the bleachers—that I know—and this wood is old enough that he might have sat here. I like to believe it, anyway.

People come in singles and pairs, and many I recognize. One heavy guy in his fifties, maybe sixties, brings a binder for baseball cards and sorts through piles of them during the game, sliding them into plastic sheets. Another has a radio in a brown, suitcaselike contraption bound with black tape. I can imagine its tubes and fuses; no microchips in there. He's tuned to Harwell and at times he stands and yells furiously, pointing toward the plate as if someone is there registering his complaints.

I like the wood bench. I lean on the wall behind it and allow my hand to fall inconspicuously onto the wood, which warms to the touch and feels smooth. In these final weeks I find myself touching this place a lot. In the dugout I rub the glossy blue walls, as I used to rub my son's back when he'd awaken from a nightmare and call out for me. He doesn't call out anymore. Recently I came early to a game and knelt at home plate, feeling the hard rubber, the color of oatmeal. I've rubbed my hands in the dirt and I've walked through the concourse with my palm on the concrete walls. Several times I've touched the flagpole in center. It's been here since day one and it's bumpy from countless coats of paint.

It reminds me—and I hesitate to admit this, knowing the inappropriateness of the analogy—how in my mother's final days I caressed her swollen right arm and laid my cheek on her forehead and just held her hand in mine as the ventilator pumped and the snow fell outside and the Christmas lights twinkled in the distance, welcoming someone else's bright holiday.

—— **Detroit 14** ◇ **Texas 6** ——

Dave Borkowski, the local kid, starts strong but loses the lead on back-to-back homers and gets pulled with the game tied.

**Game 69: Wednesday, September 1** ◇ Before fans arrive, before players take the field for practice, Al Kaline stands alone in front of the dugout, looking out toward right for the longest time. There is no one there but he sees something. By 5:34, four minutes after the gates open, Kaline is off the field and out of sight.

—— **Texas 14** ◇ **Detroit 7** ——

Jeff Weaver fails to hold a 5–1 lead.

Mom and Dad
in the 1940s.

Mom never cared for baseball, never even stepped inside the ballpark. But between surgeries she would come to my games and watch from the front seat of our paneled station wagon, staring through her black-rimmed glasses, her shaven head wrapped in a padded red scarf that didn't conceal the fresh scar that ended on her forehead. She couldn't sit in the stands for fear that a foul ball would find her vulnerable skull.

She was an artist and our basement was her studio. It smelt of turpentine and was filled with oil canvasses and watercolors of dappled riverbanks and forests of white birch and even portraits, one of me propped on a baseball bat, another of

Dad staring out the rainy window of the home on Montlieu Street.

If we live long enough, we reach the stage where our parents are no longer the first couples on the dance floor, where the weddings are for our children, not theirs, and we see their friends and their brothers and sisters disappear, claimed by one ugly disease after another.

By December of 1996 two of the people I treasured most had died.

Uncle Teddy, the dimpled defender of Santa Claus, passed in 1990. That final winter I visited him in the hospital with Dad. He had heart trouble, colon cancer, and a colostomy bag that, more than the first two, zapped his spirit for life. His room was dark and he was elevated in his bed, out of place in a gown.

"What do you think of this Larry Sheets?" I asked.

Days earlier, the Tigers had obtained the outfielder from Baltimore.

"Washed up," my uncle said. He said it with little enthusiasm, his face lacking a disdainful expression, his voice without its characteristic exuberance and *rat-a-tat* rhythm. You could hardly hear his Polish accent, which was unusual, for unlike his brothers, Uncle Teddy sounded like his pa. Most people lose their accents with time but Uncle Teddy's had grown more pronounced because his wife's family spoke Polish and he spent considerable time with them.

The Tigers were coming off their miserable 1989 season, having finished thirty games out of first place, and now they were trying to patch together a tolerable team with guys left over from the '84 championship squad and imported players like Sheets, whose best years were behind him. We both recognized the Sheets deal for what it was: a futile long shot not worth a whole lot of conversation.

"They're not giving Sparky much to work with," I said, trying to tease my uncle into an argument. I admired Sparky Anderson but my uncle was no fan, and the surest way to rile him was to praise the white-haired manager; even that failed, though. He just shrugged.

Perhaps it sounds sad that the best I could manage on that hospital visit was innocent chatter about baseball, an innocuous trade, and an upcoming season that we all suspected Uncle Teddy would not live to see. Maybe I should have attempted a deep, heart-to-heart talk. But that was not our relationship. Baseball was what connected us. It was the language we shared.

It was different with Uncle Clem, the former bohemian who had wanted to be a writer but ended up at a trucking company. He talked not only of Charlie Gehringer, but of FDR's Brain Trust and Diego Rivera's frescoes and he savored libraries and museums and volunteered his time at both. Clements Maximilian Stone, the Stankiewicz patriarch, never spent a day in college but he was more worldly and better-rounded than most of my professors. At times he could be overbearing and adamant with unwanted advice. When his youngest brother, Tom, who had been considering the priesthood, married Sandy, a former nun, Uncle Clem took it upon himself to lecture them about sex. "You're not going to live as a nun and a priest," he said.

Uncle Clem softened with age. Every Christmas he took a cross-state Greyhound bus to Detroit to spend the holiday with us. He looked like a philosopher with his piercing eyes, contemplative poses, and untamed gray beard. He knew it and he loved it. Before his arrival he would ship a dozen boxes to our home. They contained musty books that he had recovered from the stacks at St. Vincent de Paul, where he gave his time on Wednesdays, organizing an extensive section that would shame some small libraries. He believed that everyone, no matter how poor, should own books. In December he would send us books we liked and books he thought we should like. He sent me a biography of Ty Cobb, a collection of Red Smith, and over time, four copies of Hemingway's *The Old Man and the Sea*. After Uncle Clem died in 1993 I read it.

Uncle Clem believed that travel made a person whole, and he tried to encourage journeys by giving French, Italian, Greek, Russian, and Spanish translation dictionaries. He liked that I was a writer but he hoped journalism would lead to something more meaningful, like fiction or poetry. Many of his friends became authors and artists. But it was a young man on Montlieu Street, Joseph Spencer, stricken by tuberculosis, who became his life's passion. Beezie, as they called him, spent long afternoons in his upstairs bedroom, sketching the scenes that developed outside in the alley behind Montlieu, doing washes and woodcuts from his window. Beezie lived until 1940, age twenty-five. But for a half century after, Uncle Clem would tell anyone who might listen about his talented friend.

I was in Michigan's Upper Peninsula when Uncle Clem died suddenly, days before his eightieth birthday. I was with my Air Force friend Mike Varney and we had a beer in my uncle's honor.

I've worked at weekly newspapers for twenty years. If I've learned anything, it's that our lives aren't about the big stories that shape history; they're about the little ones that play themselves out in the places we treasure—homes, schools, and ballparks—and with the people we hold dear.

For nine days in December 1996, Mom lay in room 5811 of the intensive-care unit at William Beaumont Hospital. She had brain and bone cancer and her life was coming to an end. Some days Dad would be filled with hope, drawn to a single optimistic word in a doctor's otherwise dismal report, drawn like a cat to the dancing rays of a twisting prism.

I asked a friend whose own mother had died years before: "How do you deal with the loss?"

"I don't," he said.

Uncle Herb.

**Game 70: Thursday, September 2** ◇ "Hi, every-body. Baseball greetings from The Corner. Beauuuu-ti-fullll afternoon here at Michigan and Trumbull, Tiger Stadium, and the Detroiters are entertaining the Texas Rangers. It'll be game number four, the final game of the series, the final game of the current home stand for the Tygs, and they lead the Rangers two games to one. Jim Price is with us and he's got those line-ups. . . ."

It's just after one P.M. and Ernie Harwell, Price, and engi-neer Howard Stitzel have settled into their tiny eight-by-eight booth above and to the right of home plate. It is as plain as a Mennonite's closet. The two broadcasters sit at a narrow counter, papers scattered about it, with a garbage basket between them and a bare bulb in a socket taped to the ledge in front. Harwell's on an ordinary folding chair, his Detroit Stars Negro League cap dropped onto the 1960s tiled floor, along with his mail. He has stuck a team schedule to the wall.

When I began this adventure in April, I had not met Ernie Harwell. He did not know me or about my mission or this book. Within that first week, recognizing that I was new and perhaps seeing that I felt out of place, he approached me, extended his hand, and offered assistance.

"A journalist?" he said, reading my business card. "Isn't that someone who wears spats?"

He once escorted me into the visitors' clubhouse to introduce Travis Fryman and Frank Tanana. As the season progressed, he always nodded a smile, frequently asked about the project, inquired about my luck in finding a publisher, even offered advice. For the longest while, he called me "Bookman," probably because he had forgotten my name. Now he calls me Tom.

On the air Harwell says, "It's a strike. Mr. Eddings said so. It cut right through the heart of the plate. . . . Mr. Gonzalez stood there like the house by the side of the road and watched that one go by."

Seventy-some years ago Harwell was a Georgia boy taking elocution lessons from a Mrs. Margaret Lackland. No one could have imagined then that he would make his living talking.

"I couldn't say 'chicken,' for instance. It would come out 'ficken.' Or 'sister' would be 'fister.' It was not quite a lisp but what they called, unscientifically, 'tongue-tied.' We had to make speeches and debate every month in the public schools. Mrs. Lackland helped me overcome it. She just died about a year or two ago in Albany, Georgia. I kept in touch with her."

Mrs. Lackland had Ernie memorize poems like "Christopher

Columbus," "Horatio at the Bridge," and Sam Walter Foss's "The House by the Side of the Road," from which Harwell subconsciously adapted his trademark expression.

But it was his dad, Davis Gray Harwell, who taught him the sport.

"He was a great baseball fan," says Harwell. "He worked at a furniture store. He'd come home and I'd run up to meet him and he'd have the paper. They used to have the special sports editions with the final scores. We didn't have radio then. So I'd find out if the Atlanta Crackers won or lost. He had a good friend who was a big-league pitcher, Sherrod Smith, who pitched for Brooklyn and Cleveland, and they were from the same hometown. My dad used to go up to Chicago for the furniture mart. He'd always see Sherrod. He'd go down and sit in the dugout with him. They were pretty close."

After multiple sclerosis debilitated his dad's legs, the younger Harwell went to games with neighbors and uncles.

For sixty years he has been broadcasting, starting with his Crackers and moving on to the Brooklyn Dodgers, New York Giants, and Baltimore Orioles before George Kell recommended him for the Tigers job. He has been in Detroit since 1960.

"To anyone growing up here, Ernie Harwell was the last thing you heard before your eyes closed at night," a photographer, Mark Cunningham, told me earlier this year.

Getting to know Harwell, even a little bit, has been one of the highlights of my season. Sometimes idols do live up to your expectations. Over and over this year, two names have surfaced repeatedly in conversation with fans: Al Kaline and Ernie Harwell.

"I'm flattered to be bracketed with Kaline," Harwell said before the game. "I don't know whether I deserve that or not. We do hear from a lot of people who tell me that they grew up listening to the transistor and hiding it from their mom under the pillow. Things like that. There are a lot of stories that get multiplied over the years. I really can't take any credit.

"I think it's mainly because the announcer in every region is always a conduit between the team and the public. Any radio baseball announcer who comes into an area and stays there four or five years, whether he's good or bad, begins to fulfill that role. They get used to you. It's sort of like the old slipper. It might not be as good as the new one but it fits a little better. The warmth and the affection they've shown me, whether deserved or not, is something I deeply appreciate. It makes me feel very humble that people care that much."

Never was it so evident as when Harwell got fired in 1991. The team and radio station wanted a new direction. They unceremoniously dumped Harwell.

The winter before he died, Uncle Clem zipped off an angry letter about such corporate callousness. "What is happening?" he wrote. "They have dropped the word 'human' out of 'human being.'"

The firing was unpopular.

"It was something that happens in a lot of businesses," Harwell said. "I realize that it wasn't anything unique. It was just something that happened to me. I've always felt that things happen for the better and I believe in this case that it happened for the better. In the long run as I look back, it was probably a good thing for me and my career. Just from a professional standpoint, it gave me a little more publicity and projected me into the limelight a little more. When I got fired, they had some special editions in the paper and a lot of people wrote in and said nice things. What really touched me was what Sara Simpson [who operates the press elevator] told me: 'You know, most people have to die to have things like that said about them. You're lucky that you're still alive and that you can read and hear those things.' It was very touching to me and something I will never forget."

Before the game, as we sat and chatted near the on-deck circle, fans approached for autographs and photos.

"Do you mind if I take your picture, Mr. Harwell?" asked one.

"Go right ahead," he said. "Do you want me to look at the camera?"

"No, just go on talking."

Harwell turned to me and continued.

"I've spent as much time in that booth in the summer as I have at home," he said. "It's very comfortable for me. I love the people around here. I like the concessionaires. I know a lot of them. I see them almost every time I come out. And the ushers, of course, the players and the clubhouse workers and everybody connected with the whole thing. To me it's sort of like coming to a party every day. You walk around, you see everybody, and they're nice and friendly and warm and respectful. I just enjoy coming. I really do.

"I'll miss the fact that we're so close to the field," he added. "I think that's a great plus here that we'll never get at the other ballpark. We're right up close. That's the distinguishing feature to me. The closeness of the stands and the fans to the players. It's enhanced by the fact that we have the upper deck all around and I think that gives you a feeling that you're even closer than you probably actually are. I don't have any complaints about it. I know the fans have problems with getting in the bathroom and the long lines to the concession stands and the obstructed views. Those seem to be the big objections but I'm a little luckier than most because I've got a free seat and a good view and free food. I don't worry about those things.

"I don't mind the antiquated parts," Harwell said. "I don't mind that the clubhouse is crowded and old-fashioned and that the hot water gives out in the visitors' clubhouse. That doesn't concern me so much. I empathize with those guys but it doesn't bother me a whole lot. I like it here. I guess if there was one complaint that I could conjure up it would probably be the weather in April. But I can't do anything about that. It's awful windy and cold here some April nights when they want to play baseball. I don't like baseball in the cold weather."

I looked forward to those early-April games the way most kids looked forward to birthdays. I awaited Ernie Harwell's voice, a harbinger of spring, a voice that still melts snow.

—— **Detroit 8** ◇ **Texas 7** ——

Bobby Higginson leads with two homers, including one that starts a rally.

The author.
Photo by my
dad, Joe
Stanton.

**Game 71: Friday, September 10** ◇ As a boy I
wrote fawning letters to ballplayers, in envelopes striped with
color markers. In return I'd get photos autographed by Bruce
Kimm and Manny Sanguillen and on occasion an Aaron or
Clemente. At the least I'd receive a team schedule and maybe a
decal.

The Tigers, whom I inundated with letters, put me on a
mailing list and every winter sent a flyer advertising season
tickets. At twelve, with Dad cashing savings bonds to help pay
for Mom's surgeries, I realized it was a luxury we could not
afford. At best we'd see three or four games a year, usually

with tickets from Uncle Teddy, who had connections. We never hit double digits and any thought of going to all eighty-one games would be dismissed as quickly as Bobby Riggs had been. Still, I dreamed of a time when I'd see all of them (and eat Snickers bars for dinner and buy Topps cards by the box and be free of Jim Albright, a bigger kid who used to punch my arm and chase me home from school).

Eventually I got my wish—the first one, anyway. I now share tickets with several other men. For five seasons our seats have been between home and third in section 217, row D, numbers 5, 6, 7, and 8. Elmore Leonard's section. These are the seats that Beth and my boys have tonight and I sit beside them.

When you have a season's pass, you begin to recognize the fans around you: the guy in his forties with the waxed moustache—I call him Rollie Fingers—who always brings two bags of peanuts and gives one away; the young man with hunched shoulders and a briefcase stocked with sharp pencils and team rosters, who watches intently, listens on a Walkman, and scratches out plays on a scoresheet; and the bearded fellow who collects autographs and raises his latest find, maybe a ticket signed by Gregg Jefferies, toward the fourth man, with dour face and arms eternally crossed over his belly, who nods his approval, like Marlon Brando in *The Godfather*.

Last year the one with the moustache, Rollie Fingers, gave my boys a bag of peanuts and I felt as if I were on the verge of cracking the clique. This year I rarely see the four together, and tonight only the bearded one is here. My boys used to trade smiles when they'd spot those men. They found it funny that these guys would come alone to almost every game.

It's less funny now that their father does the same thing.

Though my sons enjoy baseball, none of them loves it as I did.

They don't scrape together neighborhood kids for summer-morning games or rearrange their schedules to see the Tigers on television or refrain from swimming for fear of tightening their throwing arms.

Of my boys, Taylor, ten, likes baseball least. Tonight he occupies himself with the video camera, pretending to be his idol, Steven Spielberg. Taylor played for a team this summer with William, his twin brother. It was probably Taylor's last year of organized ball.

Zack, fourteen, has never played. He follows the sport and always accepts an invitation to the ballpark, and he knows that Derek Jeter grew up in Kalamazoo and that Greg Maddux won four straight Cy Young awards and that ninety-six lights are on the tower over first base. Sometimes I wonder if he shows interest just for me.

Of my boys, it is William who most loves baseball.

"Will you play catch?" he always asks after school.

The other day during a family picnic in our yard, Willie got our gloves and a ball. As most of his uncles and aunts and cousins talked and ate on the deck, he threw fastballs. He's a lefty and he likes me to crouch down like a catcher and call balls and strikes. I did until my knees tired.

He returned the favor and gave me a target.

"This is Denny McLain," I said, kicking my left leg up and out, like a Radio City Rockette.

The ball hit Willie's mitt.

"This is Mark Fidrych." I talked to the ball, snaked my arm toward the plate, as if casting a spell, and pulled my bent leg toward my chest.

Willie laughed.

By now Dad was leaning against the deck's railing and watching the two of us.

I threw one underhand, submarine style.

"Who's that?" Willie asked.

His grandpa beamed.

"Good old Elden Auker," Dad said.

—— **Detroit 7** ◇ **Toronto 6** ——

Detroit comes from behind with four runs in the eighth. Juan Encarnacion wins it on a single.

**Game 72: Saturday, September 11** ◇ I could interview the newlyweds who dropped by the park to have pictures taken or I could talk to Toronto fans who drove hours and crossed an international border to get here. But I'd rather not. These final days are growing more personal and I find myself protecting my time, preferring to spend it with family, friends, and the regulars I've gotten to know.

Before the game I scoop a vial of dirt from near the dugout and watch Al Kaline and Alan Trammell with pitcher David Wells. They're laughing and shoulder-patting and they look happy to see each other.

Ernie Harwell greets me by name as he passes.

I see Amzie Griffin, the concessionaire with the immaculate fingernails. He's battling a late-summer cold. "I hate colds," he says. He holds up the newest sweatshirt, somberly imprinted with *The Final Farewell*. A while back I had introduced my sons to him and he lectured them briefly. "Your daddy's not always going to support you. Get an education," he said.

And there's Michael Litaker, the high-school English teacher with unfashionably long hair who freelances as a photographer, and Art, the dog vendor, doffing his cap, and Marty Taft up high in Al the Usher's section with his old ball glove, the color of molasses.

Marty, who has two tickets to every Tigers home game, grew up in New York, a Brooklyn Dodgers fan. He was a teenager when Walter O'Malley moved the team to California. If you were to visit Taft's home, you'd find a three-foot model of Ebbets Field, along with art prints and other memorabilia.

"My fondest hope," he told me months ago, "is that Walter O'Malley is really, really warm today. I mean really crisp."

The Dodgers left Ebbets Field forty-two years ago.

—— **Toronto 9** ◇ **Detroit 5** ——

The Blue Jays hammer Willie Blair.

**Game 73: Sunday, September 12** ◇ The players have been herded from the clubhouse into the dugout and a few are grumbling because they're about to be sent to the edge of the warning track, where hordes of fans will snap their pictures in the hot sun.

"This is Mickey Mouse," says one.

The photo session follows an on-field baseball clinic for children. There was a mini-clinic the day before. Some players have tired of these marketing efforts.

Robert Fick, a wiry rookie with a pale complexion, complains that's he not in the lineup again. "Why did they bring me up?" he asks. He has missed most of the year with a shoulder injury and he wants to play.

Upstairs in the press box, Joe Falls collects the lineups,

game-day information, and sheets of statistics that the team makes available.

"Hello," he says, his voice warm, not caustic.

Weeks ago I abandoned any thought of chatting meaningfully with the guy who had inspired me to write.

"Hello, Mr. Falls," I respond.

"It's Joe," he says. "Joe."

For a moment I think maybe I should make the effort.

But I don't. I wander off, saying nothing more.

The baseball has been pitiful this year. I had hoped the Tigers would surprise everyone with a wild-card playoff berth, an American League pennant, or a miraculous world championship. When it became obvious they lacked the talent, I wished that Gabe Kapler or Jeff Weaver would emerge as stars and battle for Rookie of the Year honors. That didn't happen, either. Then I wished the team would lose the most games in history, a curse of sorts. Now I'm trying to will an event of substance, an on-field achievement, an individual performance to mark this season in history, to make it unforgettable. Maybe a perfect game.

Today I vow not to leave the press box until Jeff Weaver puts a runner on base. It doesn't take long. He gets two quick outs in the first inning, walks a batter, hits the next one, walks another, and surrenders a two-run double. No perfect game. No no-hitter. No shutout. Not even a victory.

I have a friend who sees Bob Dylan as a luminous soul, and another who mocks his muddled words. Periodically, the one tries to convince the other of Dylan's brilliance, offering the evidence of his influence, explaining the poetry and the 1960s, and growing more emphatic and frustrated as he goes on because the other guy just doesn't get it, doesn't get Dylan. I suspect it's that way with this stadium and my affection for it. Some people don't understand.

Maybe I'm wrong to wish for a momentous event. Isn't it

enough that our grand ballpark is dying? Doesn't that fact alone give this final season importance? Should it just go silently into our hearts?

—— **Toronto 5** ◇ **Detroit 3** ——

Jeff Weaver loses despite two home runs and a double by Deivi Cruz.

◇ ◇ ◇ ◇ ◇ ◇ *The Last Home Stand*

Alan Trammell and Tony LaRussa.

**Game 74: Monday, September 20** ◇ Pete Munoz's anger toward Ken Griffey Jr. has dissipated.

"He wouldn't sign my *Sports Illustrated*, you know. But it's all right."

Munoz adjusts his backward Indians cap.

"I brought the magazine. He wouldn't sign it," he says. "I saw him and I was trying to hurry up to open it. But he was gone. It's all right. I was watching ESPN and they said he wouldn't be signing no autographs or nothing because he's just thinking about hitting home runs and trying to catch up to Mark McGwire and Sammy Sosa."

"Did you find a ticket yet for the final game?"

"Ah, my friend didn't come through," Pete says. "He told me, 'Don't worry about it. I'll get you a ticket.' So I don't go buy one."

His friend gave the ticket to someone else.

"I'm gonna still come down. I'll hang around, watch the TV at the bar. There's a lot of them around here. I love coming down. I love coming to this stadium. No matter whether the Tigers win or lose, I still come. Right now Tiger Stadium looks beautiful. It's all around," he says, waving his gloved hand. "It's my house. I just love coming here. I must tell you that many times."

I wish I had a ticket to give Pete. Anyone who's been sitting in the cheap seats for dozens of games each year over several decades shouldn't be cut out of the final game. If I had an extra ticket, I would give it to him. We shake hands and I thank Pete for his company this year.

"See you at the new park," he says.

I find my dad near the visitors' bullpen, next to a fun-loving group and its leader, Doug, who offers to buy me a beer. Doug teases the first-time ball boy, Kwame, cajoles the singing hot-dog vendor into performing, and conducts cheers for Cleveland pitchers. He also starts a wave that takes on the fifth try and spreads around the park.

Dad and I talk and our conversation drifts between baseball and family. Eventually I tell him how my relationship with Zack is changing, how Zack is distancing himself. I don't tell him how this pains me. In fact, I laugh about it. I laugh as if it doesn't hurt.

"Every teenager goes through that," he says. "They're trying to show their independence. It's good they do that. Zack's an extremely smart kid. I always told your mom when each of you turned into a teenager, 'We're going to lose them for a few years but they'll come back and figure we're not too dumb.' All kids do that. You probably don't remember."

"I remember telling you not to jingle the change in your pocket. Do you recall that?"

"Oh yeah," he says. "They come back."

He looks at me as if I'm proof.

—— **Detroit 4** ◇ **Cleveland 3** ——

After Todd Jones gives up the tying run in the ninth, the Tigers win in the tenth on a Juan Encarnacion single. Dean Palmer gets his thirty-fifth home run.

**Game 75: Tuesday, September 21** ◇ The leaves have begun changing on the tall maples outside my home. Autumn's approach shows in the golds and gray-blues of a September sky.

It's the fifth inning and Cleveland's ahead 2–0. I can't tell you how or why. Out in the lower left-field grandstands, it's easy to feel removed from the game, especially sitting twenty-six rows up on an evening like this one with the park half-empty. You can stretch your legs over the seats in front of you and extend your arms sideways and still be thirty feet from anyone.

The sun never touches this section, shaded by the second deck, which along with the posts that brace it frames a view that includes the left fielder and, in the distance, the full infield with pitcher, batter, and catcher. If the batter hits a high fly, you can't see the ball in flight because of the deck. Instead you watch where the outfielder goes. If he races toward the warning track, you know it might be a home run. If he waits patiently, glove up, tracing the ball's descent, it's probably an out.

As the sky darkens, the brightness from the lit field silhou-ettes the posts and the mesh of the fence. The concourse behind you glows an uneven yellow and the concrete beneath your feet, stained by decades of shoe dirt and spilt beer and who-knows-what-else, dissolves into a murky blackness, like a deep river on a starless night.

In a still moment you hear voices across the park. The war-bling of Charley Marcuse, the seventeen-year-old singing ven-dor with hair like Harpo Marx, travels four hundred feet over the field. Earlier he told me what he likes about this ballpark.

"It's the space," he said.

The character of the space changes depending on where you sit. Looking down from the upper deck in right, the park seems snug and small, the space intimate, hugged by the sta-dium's walls. Sitting low behind the dugout, the park appears huge, rising from the ground, its decks stacked and the light grids bolting from its roof, all of it towering above you and erupting into the endless sky.

As a teenager, when I needed space, I found refuge in the basement of our home under the shiny cone of a vanilla-Naugahyde hair dryer, a remnant of Mom's beauty salon. The cone lowered over your head and blew hot air onto your scalp, whispering on your tingling neck, an imaginary lover. The rushing air quieted the noises of our household and left me alone with my thoughts, comfortable in the subdued shaft of light emanating from the stairway.

It gave me the same solace I feel tonight, stretched out in the grandstands.

—— **Cleveland 6 ◇ Detroit 1** ——

Dave Borkowski pitches well, allowing six hits over eight innings.

**Game 76: Wednesday, September 22** ◊ Sara Simpson, somewhere in her sixties, has a creamy, chocolate complexion, hair about the color of Marilyn Monroe's, and a disposition sweet enough to make jaded journalists smile. For seventeen years she's operated the press elevator that lurches to the restricted top floor. Along the way she's come to know baseball's biggest media personalities and they've mentioned her in print and on the air. She's also gotten to know the players.

A few years back, one of them, Texas outfielder Juan Gonzalez, bought her a gift, an electric fan. It cools the stuffy elevator in which she sits most of the day. Now rumors are afloat that the Tigers want to acquire Gonzalez, one of the league's top hitters. The problem: Gonzalez doesn't want Detroit.

Before earning her seat in the elevator, Sara worked as a washroom attendant serving players' wives and kids. Since 1968 she's not missed a season, except for part of 1994, when she had heart surgery. The striking Tigers, as it turned out, missed much of that year anyway.

This seasonal stadium job is her only one. Presumably the new ballpark will have an elevator that doesn't need an attendant. No one has told her whether she will be back in 2000.

"I hope so," says Sara in her rich, unhurried manner. "It's good to be around people."

On the ball field, photographer Bill Eisner takes a photo of Ernie Harwell with the rock group the Verve Pipe, which neither one recognizes. A few members of the Michigan band seem thrilled to be on the diamond. Two others exhibit distant, unimpressed profiles, their backs to the fans, cell phones to their ears, consumed in conversations that say they are much too busy for this.

But they sing a traditional, harmonic version of the National Anthem, and pitcher Brian Moehler draws his dad's initials onto the mound and the game is under way.

From afar the crowd looks like a nubby, flecked blanket, no pattern to the colors. Up close you hear the guy in front booing Roberto Alomar for spitting on the umpire three years ago and you hear the vendor talking about where he buys tasty ribs and another guy telling where he parks for free and someone else regretting a fantasy-league draft pick.

And there's Matt Wojcik, confessing that he won't be spending a night at the ballpark. No forbidden sleepovers. "I never got around to it," he says. "The schedule didn't work out. I kind of regret it now."

When this last home stand concludes, Wojcik will have seen five of the final eight games. "It's not the baseball at this point," he says. "It's all about the stadium. Baseball's an afterthought. It's all the history that's here."

By midgame, with Damion Easley at bat, Wojcik and I notice the camera flashes. Every pitch to a Tiger is accompanied by a half dozen bursts of light. As the days wind down, the flashes increase.

"It won't all set in until next April when they actually don't play here no more," he says. "I tried to get my dad down here. He could care less. He said, 'Ah, demolish it.' He took me to my first game but he's only been here for about two or three more games.

"This is the last time you can experience baseball pretty much in its surroundings. This is it. You know, jobs change, girlfriends change, friends change, but you come here and it's pretty much the same thing. It's a constant in Detroit and it's a constant in your life. Friends come and go. This is here."

—— Cleveland 9 ◇ Detroit 1 ——

Brian Moehler gets his league-worst sixteenth loss.

**Game 77: Thursday, September 23** ◇ Zack and I are by the bullpen. Just the two of us. A few kids in the deck above are spitting over the railing at the people below.

"Zack, what do you think you'll remember most about this place?"

An almost-full moon hangs over Michigan Avenue.

I want Zack to say he'll remember us coming together, he'll remember his grandpa, my uncles Teddy and Clem, his brothers and his mom and my brother and our friends. Mostly, in my greedy little mind, I want him to say that he'll remember me.

He struggles for an answer.

"The shape of the outfield," he says.

And then he adds, "One of the things I like about this stadium is that when it's rainy the expensive seats get wet."

Well, at least I know he's a Democrat.

—— **Detroit 7** ◇ **Cleveland 5** ——

The Tigers rally in the fifth against the first-place Indians.

**Game 78: Friday, September 24** ◇ I've never seen so many police. Two dozen squad cars are parked along Trumbull Avenue and officers patrol on horses, waltzing past the Ty Cobb plaque where fans get their photos taken. Around here in 1984 the World Series celebration turned ugly. A car was overturned and torched. Fans rioted. Officials worry privately about trouble at the final game; publicly, they downplay the possibility.

"You don't dance on your grandmother's grave," says Tyler Barnes, the PR director.

In the parking lot Howard Stone has his own concerns. His

head cocked sideways, he rants about police threats to ticket lot owners who gouge fans.

"Don't they have anything better to do?" says Stone. He will charge $30 a space, more than usual but less than the $50 others are considering. "If I have a spot and you don't want to pay for it, don't."

Inside the park pre-game ceremonies are about to begin. This weekend the ball club is honoring its legends and trying to triumphantly close an era of baseball at this corner. The announcers say farewell tonight. George Kell, Al Kaline, and Ernie Harwell are the three most popular. Kell arrived in the mid-1940s, Kaline in the 1950s, both as players, and Harwell in 1960. Together they've touched fans for more than half a century.

The tunnels are clogged with people on the way to their seats when the retired Kell, seventy-seven, steps to the microphone.

"It's great to be back," he says with a touch of Arkansas drawl. "I got a tear when I left this city. I got another when I flew in." Around me, men in their thirties, forties, and fifties stand and applaud the third baseman. Some don't bother to wipe their eyes.

They stay standing for Harwell.

"God has given me a lot of blessings in life," he says, "and one of them has been to put me at the corner of Michigan and Trumbull."

After it's all done, after they've departed the field and before the first pitch, Al Green's aching 1971 ballad "Let's Stay Together" plays over the speakers: *Whether times are good or bad or happy or sa-a-ad . . ."*

Next to me is Mark Moellering, thirty-one. Silent, with arms folded, he looks like one of those characters who walks out of the cornstalks in *Field of Dreams*. Moellering wears a

1901 replica uniform with *DETROIT* in arched block letters across the front of a cream-colored flannel. His black cap features a red tiger and his black socks have a single horizontal stripe. Children have asked what year he played for the team.

Moellering has been to sixty games this year, down from seventy-one last year and seventy-eight two years ago.

"When you try to come to all the games, it's hard to say one seems special," he says. "But Monday, the last game, might be different."

—— **Kansas City 7** ◇ **Detroit 3** ——

Damion Easley hits his twentieth home run. The American League's two worst teams battle for possession of last place in the Central Division. The Tigers are a half game ahead of the Royals and both are more than thirty games out of first.

**Game 79: Saturday, September 25** ◇ "Why did you get unsalted peanuts?" Zack asks.

"They're better for you."

"No one likes them," he says.

Beth, the boys, and I are in the upper deck along the left-field foul line beneath rusting white-and-gray girders that remind Beth of antique lacework. While William and Zack argue over who has had the camera longer, Taylor scores the game, marking every unused box with an *X*. For a superb play he draws the action in a Chiclet-size square.

It's tough not to feel nostalgic this weekend and I don't bother trying.

Before the game the club honored its Hall of Famers, most

of whom are deceased. Kaline, Harwell, and Kell took their bows with the ancestors of Cobb, Gehringer, Greenberg, Cochrane, Heilmann, Newhouser, Heinie Manush, and Hughie Jennings—names more magical than Houdini's, names that take me back to the family gatherings of my youth, to Mom's feasts of kielbasa and kraut, lasagna and baked beans and German potato salad and endless glasses of Faygo Rock & Rye pop, to snowy evenings in our warm house, all the spots taken on the couches, with a football game on the color console and a new first baseman's glove under the silver tree and Uncle Teddy and Uncle Clem trading stories about life on Montlieu, old ball games, and the mischief that all those decades later still got them laughing so hard that Uncle Teddy cried and wheezed, the redness of his face spreading up to his bald head. It seemed to my young ears that baseball had been as central to their lives as it was to mine.

I'd love for it to be as significant to my sons.

"Hey, guys, you see the flagpole in center?" I wait for my boys to look. "That pole was here when your great-grandfather came to see Ty Cobb. It was here when Grandpa Joe was a kid and he'd come to see Charlie Gehringer. It was here when he brought me to see Al Kaline and it's still here."

I expect Zack to make a snide comment about this year's lousy team. Instead he says, "Remember that game we saw when Roger Clemens struck out twenty?" He reminisces and I feel good all through.

Afterward we linger in the stands and take our pictures—Beth and the boys, me and the boys, Beth and me—along the front-row railing, with the police and their horses on the striped field below and the seats nearly vacant, except for the others like us.

We leave through gate 9. On Cochrane Avenue Zack turns and looks back through the gate. His younger brothers pause and look, too. From the street the concourse glows orange, like embers in the ashes. It is our last game together at Tiger Stadium.

—— **Detroit 11** ◇ **Kansas City 3** ——

Brad Ausmus, with three hits, knocks in three runs.

**Game 80: Sunday, September 26** ◇ Ty Cobb's great-granddaughter, a pixie with angel hair, dances at the legs of her mother, Cindy Cobb-McGowin, a New Yorker who is seeing the park for the first time.

"It's nice to connect," she says.

She was four when her grandfather died in 1961 and of course she knows about his reputation, about the damning books and movie. But she remembers something different.

"My memories are of sitting on his lap and him reading a fairy tale to us grandkids. My grandfather was very good to his family and to a lot of people."

Today Ty Cobb is being honored as a member of the Tigers' all-time team.

In the on-deck circle is Beryl Newhouser, whose late husband Hal also made the team. "He loved his pitching," she says. "He liked his team, his teammates. He loved baseball, and when they retired his uniform here, that was one of the biggest things. He said he loved it more than anything."

I want to tell her about my dad's two hits but I tame the urge.

In the dugout another honoree, Alan Trammell, known widely as one of the nicest men in baseball, reflects on his life in the sport, all his major-league years spent in this park.

"You look at the right-field roof and think back to 1971 when I was a kid growing up and watching the All-Star game here in Detroit and watching Reggie Jackson hit that transformer. I look at that every day I come here and I'm still amazed at how far that ball was hit. I've seen a lot of home runs in my years and I still don't think I've ever seen one hit that far.

"This place just has so many memories, so much history," he says. "Sixty years ago earlier this year, Ted Williams hit the first ball over the roof. All the greats: Babe Ruth, Gehrig, Ty Cobb, Al Kaline, on and on. You can compare yourself and say, 'Heck, if they did this here, I might be able to do something like that.' To me the best way to describe Tiger Stadium is that 'it felt like baseball.'

"Growing up in San Diego, I had been there and to Anaheim Stadium and Dodger Stadium, and they're all stadiums with parking lots, with acreage. I remember the first time coming here and driving around the corner and club officials pointing out Tiger Stadium. I couldn't comprehend because I was used to seeing a big parking lot around a stadium and it isn't the case here. I kept thinking, 'How in the heck do they get 50,000 people in here and where do they park?' Well, lo and behold, they've done it for many, many years."

Trammell excuses himself and heads into the clubhouse.

Kaline, Kell, and Greenberg are on the all-time team, along with Sparky Anderson, Bill Freehan, Jack Morris, Mickey Lolich, and John Hiller, the relief pitcher whose groceries I once carried. ("No shit?" he says when I tell him the story. He rolls his eyes.)

The final spot on the team goes to Kirk Gibson.

"Kirk Gibson?" says John Ward, who had been stuffing the ballot box for Harry Heilmann and Sammy Crawford. Ward had feared that the Hall of Famers would be overlooked. Both retired before 1930 and had career averages over .300. "What a fraud. What a short memory Detroit fans have. That's ridiculous."

David Kleckner would agree. He knows his baseball, has been coming to the games since 1964, and learned about the sport from his ambidextrous grandmother, who listened to games on radio, ironing with one hand and scoring with the other.

Oh, and David Kleckner is my son's band teacher, the much-heralded Mr. Kleckner about whom Zack boasts, the same Mr. Kleckner who plays a dozen or more instruments, owns more baseball cards than I do, has a bigger record collection, and does not—it turns out—belong to Mensa.

"There's something about walking into this stadium," he says. "There's a smell, there's a feel, there's an ambience of baseball. You can't even see the field yet and you're walking through the tunnels, going up the ramps. It just has a unique feeling. You can't describe it. It's almost like all the old ballplayers are hanging around. Then when you come out and see the grass and field, you can feel the baseball permeating this place."

"You know, my son idolizes you," I tell him, not meaning to change the subject so abruptly. "He constantly brags about you."

"I went through the same thing," he says. "Your dad's not cool, your parents aren't cool." That's all the attention he gives my concern and it's enough.

"When I was a kid, I saw Willie Mays on TV," he says. "My dad would fill me in about the guys who played when he was a kid. That's how I got to know the old players. My dad just retired. He's seventy-three and lives in Iowa. All the memories are here. All the games my grandma and I watched on TV were here.

"When all the people are gone and you think back . . ." His

words drift off, the sentence unfinished. "Well, it'll take awhile to warm up to Comerica Park."

—— **Detroit 6** ◇ **Kansas City 1** ——

Dave Borkowski, the rookie from the suburbs, gets his first Tiger Stadium victory in his last appearance at the park. Rob Fick contributes a pair of hits. That's four in two days.

◇ ◇ ◇ ◇ ◇ ◇ ◇   *The Old Neighborhood*

On the drive to the ballpark Sunday morning, I turned off the interstate onto Van Dyke Avenue, one of several major roads that head out of Detroit like spokes from a hub.

Streetcars once ran here, past bright stores and sidewalks bustling with activity. It wasn't a wealthy neighborhood but it was lively and safe. Now, boarded buildings line Van Dyke, interrupted by beauty salons, pawn shops, and missionary churches with barred windows. It's the kind of place where visitors check their car-door locks and time the traffic signals to avoid stops.

Yesterday, after I passed the railroad tracks the streetscape became familiar. Lyford was on the right, bordering the hilly field where Dad played as a boy and where Uncle Teddy choked a kid until he turned blue and where Johnny Castiglione searched for chunks of coal that fell from trains. Up farther on the left was Georgia Park, the site of Dad's success against Newhouser. I passed Elgin, Wisner, and Montlieu Streets. Along the stretch would have been Temrowski's Drug Store, C. F. Smith Grocer, and Forest Lawn Bar, where Uncle Tom played war, flipping bottlecaps as his oldest brothers fought the real thing overseas. Talenda's Bowling, once a Club Crusader hangout, had become a liquor store, and next to the former Maurie's Candy Store were the skeletal remains of the greenhouse where the Stankiewicz kids had pooled their money for Grandma's Easter corsages. Nature had reclaimed the spot, twines and trees consuming the framework.

I turned right onto Nuernberg at Holy Name Church, now St. James Baptist. A security guard stood outside the wooden doors, watching parishioners' cars. Behind the church was Holy Name School, where Dad listened to the final game of the 1935 World Series, and behind that was the auditorium, now occupied by the Police Athletic League. Somewhere pinched between these buildings there had been a ball field, where Uncle Bucky challenged the unspoken church-league color barrier. In 1934, long before Jackie Robinson became a Dodger, Bucky recruited Jack George, a black teen, for Dad's squad. "Bucky was trying to get people riled up," Dad said recently. "But nobody said nothing because Jack George was a hell of a pitcher. He didn't stay on our team long. He was too good." (Incidentally, it would take another couple decades for the Tigers to put a black player on their roster.)

At Gilbo I turned and headed back toward Montlieu. There were fields where homes once stood and a hungry dog sniffing for food. There was a car on blocks and another with its hood up and a man working on the engine. There were houses, as well, one with a potted mum in a front window.

In the late 1970s Uncle Teddy moved from the neighborhood. Within days the home was stripped of bricks and siding, then set afire, the Babe Ruth cards still in the wall. Eventually its charred bones crumbled.

Uncle Clem visited at Christmas in 1985 and he asked to be driven to Montlieu Street. He needed to see for himself. As we approached, his lips tightened around a Newport cigarette and he blew smoke into rings.

"Oh, for chrissakes," he said, looking at the lot.

Fresh snow, like a coroner's white sheet, covered the land. He turned away.

"It's as if we were never here," he said.

It is discourteous—and perhaps wrong and conceited—to say that this neighborhood died when it deteriorated, when it became something different from our memories of it. Half the houses have disappeared since my father's boyhood, but families still live here. Children still walk to church in their dress clothes, though contrasted by a backdrop of vacated buildings. A colorful, molded-plastic play set accents one yard and kids probably play ball on sunny afternoons. By my eyes this area hasn't changed much in fifteen or twenty years. It wasn't the kind of place I would have chosen to live then; it's not the kind of place I would choose to live now. But I keep coming back, like the Canada geese that land each autumn near my house at a driving range that used to be a wide-open field.

Some architects say we cannot ignore the history of a property. There is memory associated with it. They compare it to a palimpsest, parchments that in Roman times were scraped and reused but retained shadows of earlier markings. Land is like that, etched by its past.

As kids we write our names on walls and carve them into trees and onto park benches. As adults we buy video cameras and commission family portraits. If we're rich, we may give money to be honored with a hospital wing, a library, or a park. Ultimately our names are marked in stone and cemented into the ground amid trees and grass. All of this for a little immortality.

It's for the same reason that we want the terrains of our youth to remain forever as we remember them. For as long as they do, a part of us also remains.

◊ ◊ ◊ ◊ ◊ ◊ ◊   *Good-byes*

Dad and I at the final game.

**Game 81: Monday, September 27** ◊ Twenty-four weeks ago, on a chilly day in April, I began this journey. Today I will complete it, having seen all eighty-one home games, including this one, the last at The Corner, Michigan and Trumbull. Sure, I could still get shot trying to keep a drunk from dismantling the ballpark or I could fall over with a heart attack in Howard Stone's parking lot. But barring tragedy I will walk through gate 9 and finish my mission.

It's almost ten A.M. and already Howard has been in his lot for five hours. He arrived before the sun cast its first long shadows of morning, before the TV trucks had pulled up. This afternoon, after the cars have been parked, he will do what he hasn't done all year: He will see a game.

"I'm going with my son-in-law," he says. "We're going to bond."

Though the gates won't open until one-thirty, a few fans have begun circling the stadium, looking protectively at the dull, blue-tiled wall as if to say, *We'll get through this together. We're right beside you.*

Inside, Amzie Griffin cleans his glass shelves and sets out merchandise.

"Thirty-nine years," he says. "All in all it's been a good run. It's going to be sad for me tonight. I like it here. As a matter of fact, I love it. I'll never say good-bye. I'll always drive by and say, 'See you later.' As you can tell, I'm getting a little emotional about it. I raised three of my children here, my two oldest boys and my youngest daughter. They worked with me and now my granddaughter does."

A busy day lies ahead for Amzie. Crowds will be enormous, lines congested, emotions high.

For the moment, though, I walk in solitude along the concourse with shafts of light sliding through slats and fences. I climb the ramps that lead to the center-field bleachers, to the top row under the scoreboard where my rose-gardening grandpa sat in the late 1930s, and then back down to the lower bleachers where I met architect John Lee Davids and Pete Munoz, who never did get Griffey's autograph, through the narrow gate that separates the cheap seats from all the others, and up the tunnel near the visitors' bullpen, dodging the worker who hoses the cement walkway; past one dugout and up the cracked steps to where Zack saw his first game and up farther to the top level, passing Mary Pletta, who readies her hot-dog grill, and over a catwalk into Al the Usher's area—he's not around yet—as team president John

McHale Jr., in red bow tie, strolls by alone and acknowledges pitcher Dave Mlicki, who pans the park with a video camera. I notice the front-row seats where Dad, Uncle Teddy, and I sat and from which I had called down to Willie Horton as a game played on the field. He was on the dugout steps and he waved back. It was my first exchange with someone whose skin was a color different from my own and it shaped me in a subtle way.

Downstairs, relief pitcher Todd Jones, in shorts and T-shirt, poses for photos with the servers who work the boxed seats. Ushers have begun to arrive, a few wearing their retired orange uniforms.

"Get your butt to the gate," Joe Falls yells at one of them. They laugh and hug in the aisle.

In section 217 in the cool shade in my usual seat, I rest my eyes on the field, most of it washed in sunlight. Near third base a worker softens the dirt with a rake. In center, a sprinkler sprays the grass, the water glistening like diamonds on green felt. Through the mist, I see the white numbers 440 on the farthest part of the outfield wall, proclaiming the exaggerated distance from home plate, daring hitters to swing for it. Soon the lines will be chalked, the bases anchored, and the plate painted white. The sight is serene and sublime and comforting, too, for in all my years of coming here the field has looked the same. The wooden seats were removed in the 1970s, the walls painted blue. The Tiger Plaza, a food court, was added in the 1990s. The park has changed some. But the grass has always been green and the flagpole has always stood in fair territory in center field.

This ballpark challenges the notion that you can never go home. For no matter how my life has evolved and how many years have passed and how far my hairline has shifted, I feel like a kid when I come here. This place awakens those spirits and allows me to reclaim parts of myself that otherwise might be lost. Here my life echoes with those of the men and boys who have meant the most to me.

We all need places like this.


I meet Mike Varney in the Tiger Plaza before the game. He drove in from Milwaukee after waking at three-twenty this morning to a wrong-number phone call from Thailand. He had not set an alarm and the call came minutes before he was due out of bed.

"I think it was my dad," he says.

"Your dad passed away in the eighties, Mike."

"Yeah, but I think he put that call in to make sure I woke up and got here on time. He wouldn't want me to miss this."

"Maybe it was my uncle Herb, with his Asian connections and all."

"No, it was my dad," he says. Neither of us has heard from Uncle Herb.

We head to our seats and find my father and brother.

The grandstand is a collage of banners, testaments of faith and friendship.

*So long, old girl*, one says.

*This will always be home*, states another.

*Baseball cries today*, on a third.

As the 4:05 start approaches, Ernie Harwell introduces Al Kaline, the greatest living Tiger, and the crowd rises for number 6, who is wearing his uniform. Kaline tips his cap and backs away from the microphone, biting his lip. The ovation continues for more than a minute. He steps forward again. The applause builds once more. Kaline bows his head and swallows hard. In the visitors' dugout Kansas City players stand and watch, joined by former third baseman George Brett, who was a rookie in 1974 when the right fielder ended his career.

Kaline recalls his first day at the park.

"I was awestruck," he says. "As a kid fresh out of high school, I suppose that was only natural. Yet today, forty-six years later, I stand before you a grown man, a veteran of thousands of games in this park, and again I find myself humbled and somewhat overwhelmed by the events unfolding in front of us."

A quiet has settled on the stadium.

"While common materials may have been used to build this place—concrete, steel, and bricks—the memories are the cement that has held it together for eighty-eight wonderful seasons. . . . Is it a specific game that you will remember most about Tiger Stadium? Maybe Ty Cobb sliding hard into third. George Kell diving to his left. Norm Cash or Kirk Gibson blasting one into the lights in right field. Or will it be a memory of your family and friends, sharing a story with your best buddy or listening closely as your dad tells you of the first time he came to the ballpark years ago?"

At game time Brian Moehler carries out his ritual on the pitching mound. Moehler is wearing Jack Morris's number, 47. Like all of our starters, he is honoring a member of the all-time team. Tony Clark wears 5 for Hank Greenberg, and Damion Easley, number 2 for Charlie Gehringer. Gabe Kapler has Cobb's numberless back—and socks that show.

In the left-field grandstand Uncle Tom wonders about Billy Rogell, who threw out the first pitch. "That man has got to be old," he says. "I used to play in the Billy Rogell Baseball League and he was old then." (Rogell, ninety-four, debuted in the majors in 1925.)

My uncle had such a grand time here in August that he insisted on coming back. He's with his son-in-law and grandson on this Monday. Clogged aisles will keep him from joining my dad today. But they ask about each other and that makes me proud.

Of all the gifts this year has brought, the best has been seeing Dad and Uncle Tom together and hearing them talk about Grandpa Stankiewicz, life on Montlieu Street, and baseball. Their rolling conversation transported me to a time when Uncle Teddy and Uncle Clem traded stories in a way that illuminated my life and made me feel part of something bigger than myself.

There is a talent to telling stories and my old uncles possessed it, though their styles differed. An actor by nature, Clem would unwind his tales like taut kitestring and they would soar. Teddy did it in such a way that you had to nudge him along with questions. At story's end he would seem as surprised as you by the outcome. Sixty years on, he still would have shock on his face as he remembered waking from surgery on the kitchen table and discovering that the family doctor had not only removed his tonsils but also his foreskin. "I knew my tonsils weren't down there," he said.

Something sad happens to memories as our loved ones die off. Our pool of stories evaporates like salted water on a stove. We remember many, of course, and we add our own. But others are lost forever. When Uncle Teddy and Uncle Clem and Mom passed on, they took a share with them and those can't be reclaimed. But to have Uncle Tom reenter our lives now allows us to replenish the supply. It also makes Dad's life a little more complete.

I've always found that places rouse memories better than songs, smells, or snapshots. A grove of birch trees in northern Michigan recalls my mom, with her easel at the riverbank and her brush moving furiously before the paper dries. The playground at Robert Frost School conjures rivalries and friendships and the time I accidentally split open Ron-Ron Mancini's head with a baseball bat during a game of 500.

Perhaps it's the same with you.

All season I've heard players and fans say that what they

will take from this park are memories. I will also. But while I've been blessed with many things in my life, a good memory is not one of them. With the ballpark closed, how long will it be before I forget the sight of William in the front row getting Lance Parrish's autograph? Or Taylor filling every square on his scoresheet? Or Zack counting the fans in the bleachers? How long, absent the view from our seats, before my sons forget our times here together?

This final game rolls into the eighth inning, the Tigers ahead 4–2.

Detroit loads the bases for Gabe Kapler. Cameras flash throughout the park in anticipation. But Kapler grounds to the pitcher for a force at home, which brings up Rob Fick, another rookie. On the first pitch Fick smacks a ball onto the roof in right field, assuring the win and earning himself a spot in Detroit baseball history.

As the crowd celebrates, Fick rounds the bases and thanks his father, Charles, who died ten months ago. "I looked up in the sky and thought of my dad," he said later. "I just know he had something to do with all of this."

Pete Munoz is in the bleachers cheering. He had no ticket but someone looked the other way as he walked through the gate.

For the last out, Todd Jones fans Carlos Beltran on a ball that bounces to the plate.

Brian Moehler gets the victory. No one leaves the park.

In the ceremony that follows, Tigers of all eras emerge in uniform one by one from the gate in center to serene orchestral music. They head out to the positions they played, unannounced, each one cheered as fans recognize a face on the scoreboard or a name on a uniform.

First Mark Fidrych, who falls to his knees on the pitcher's mound. Then Bill Freehan, the eleven-time All-Star, as resolute as a palace guard. And Dave Bergman and Dick McAuliffe and Tom Brookens and a parade of dozens more, men in their thirties and forties and on up into their eighties and nineties, some jogging, some walking, some limping, a few riding in carts.

"There's Mickey Stanley," I whisper to Dad.

He nods.

Dan Petry follows. Then a guy named Eisenstadt, whom I don't know.

Dad scrunches his face for three seconds. "Pitched in the thirties."

We name the players as they emerge as if it were a test of our worth as fans.

John Hiller, Steve Gromek, Billy Pierce . . .

This is a forgiving audience. No one stares when your eyes get wet as Willie Horton takes left field. Horton locks his hands behind his head and pulls his elbows forward, trying to keep his emotions from escaping. He came here as a boy, played high-school ball on this field, and as a star wore his uniform in the streets during the 1967 riots to appeal for calm. His heart is in this city and in this park.

It's the players I worshiped as a kid who draw my tears: Hiller, Horton, and Lolich heading out one last time.

The championship teams of '68 and '84 are well represented under these lights. But the men who played on the '35 team when Dad was a boy are mostly gone now. Greenberg, Gehringer, Goslin, Cochrane, Tommy Bridges, "Schoolboy" Rowe, Pete Fox, Marv Owen, Gee Walker, even Jo-Jo White, who presented him with that league trophy.

"That looks like Gates Brown," Dad says.

In fact it's Ron LeFlore, who has put on a lot of weight.

The man in front of me turns to his friend and shakes his head in amused embarrassment as tears trickle toward his beard.

Jack Morris, Charlie Maxwell, Gates Brown ...

This final procession is so solemn that even the drunks have quieted.

Al Kaline. Trammell and Whitaker together.

On the field ballplayers pass the Tiger Stadium flag from center to home plate, player to player, until, to my surprise, it ends up in the hands of the submarine pitcher, Elden Auker.

When men reach a certain age—seventy-seven, let's say—a difference of a year or five is no longer discernible. It's difficult to tell an eighty-one-year-old man from an eighty-four-year-old if both are healthy. Similarly, it's hard to imagine that Dad was thirteen when Auker made it to the Tigers in 1933. There is a ten-year difference in age, yet they look like peers.

"Each of us has touched this flag today as Tiger Stadium has touched each of us. Take this flag to Comerica Park, your new home," Auker says to catcher Brad Ausmus, pausing for Comerica's boos to subside. "And take with it the boyhood dreams, the perseverance, and the competitive desire it takes to become a Detroit Tiger. Never forget us, for we live on by those who carry on the Tiger tradition and who so proudly wear the Old English *D*."

My dad is beside me in his Tiger ball cap.

Over this half year I've struggled to make sense of this season, to understand my need to be here and my attachment to this field where men play a child's game. I am beginning to understand and, oddly, I owe some of that understanding to Elden Auker. I never would have guessed it in April.

Auker was a fair pitcher, not the best on the team. He played ten years in the big leagues, never won twenty games, and his earned-run average was often near 5. Back in late June, appearing on the mound before a game, he provided an

epiphany. I saw my father in him and I started to realize and
have come to confirm, with Auker before me and Dad beside
me, why I've been drawn to this mission. It's almost as if,
twenty-seven years ago, by mimicking Auker's underhand
delivery when we played catch in our yard, Dad set this year
in motion, that he was preparing me for the final season.

I've noticed something today. It's not the seventy- and
eighty-year-old men who are wiping their eyes. It's the generations that came after them. And we're hurting not only for
the loss of this beautiful place, but for the loss of our fathers
and grandfathers—belatedly or prematurely. The closing of
this park forces us to confront their mortality, and when we
confront their mortality we must confront our own. If the
park is here, part of my dad will always be here, as will a part
of me. A little bit of us dies when something like this, something so tied to our lives, disappears. This season has helped
me realize that my life is becoming more like the stories of my

Harold
"Prince Hal"
Newhouser.
Photo
courtesy
of Burton
Historical
Collection,
Detroit
Public
Library.

father and my uncles, set in places that exist only in memory. In my perfect world Tiger Stadium would be as I've always remembered it and it would remain long after I'm gone, to help my boys remember me.

After his friend Johnny Castiglione passed away, Dad delivered another in a lifetime of lessons: We live on through our attachments to people, through our relationships with the ones we love.


The ballpark has nearly cleared as we take a slow walk to gate 9, looking at the overhang and at Newhouser's number 16 and at the green of the field.

"Are you all right, Dad?" I ask, rubbing his shoulders.

"Oh yeah," he says. "How about you?"

"I think so."

I lay a red rose near the dugout for Grandpa, and we head off into the night.

—— **Detroit 8 ◇ Kansas City 2** ——

◇ ◇ ◇ ◇ ◇ ◇   *A Year Later*

Comerica Park opened April 11, 2000, on a day when they had to shovel snow from the field, the kind of day that Ernie Harwell says wasn't made for baseball. Brian Moehler pitched the home opener, putting his father's initials into the new dirt, and the Tigers won 5–2. And I can say I was there with 39,000 others, shivering in the cold wind.

It's August now and I've seen a half dozen games this season including this one, a Tuesday-night affair against the Griffeyless Seattle Mariners.

Much has changed since the last game at Tiger Stadium. Days before the Yankees swept the World Series in October, Detroit fired manager Larry Parrish and replaced him with

Phil Garner, a guy nicknamed "Scrap Iron." In their quest to add a star to the lineup, the club sent Gabe Kapler, Justin Thompson, Francisco Cordero, Frank Catalanotto, and Bill Haselman to Texas for Juan Gonzalez and others. Gonzalez, who can become a free agent this year, has already rejected a contract estimated at over $120 million, and Kapler has settled into center field with the Rangers, stringing together a twenty-eight-game hitting streak. I suspect we will regret trading him. An even greater travesty, though, is that Garner could not justify a coaching position for Alan Trammell, who had hoped to spend his career in one uniform. Instead he wears Padre colors.

Tonight's lineup features five hitters who started last year. Luis Polonia and Karim Garcia have departed and Tony Clark and Rob Fick are injured. The standouts have been relief pitcher Todd Jones, who leads the American League in saves, and Bobby Higginson, the fan favorite who has returned to form. Jeff Weaver continues to develop, and hometown boy Dave Borkowski may get another shot in September. After a slow start, the team appears within reach of .500 and attendance has jumped. The park has been filled seventeen times.

In my visits to this new place, I have found Amzie Griffin, the concessionaire with shiny nails, hawking programs at a small stand, and have learned that Sara Simpson still operates the press elevator. I have seen Bill Eisner snapping his photos and have spotted other familiar faces, too. Art Witkosky may be selling hot dogs and Al the Usher may be protecting his seats but I've yet to find them.

Comerica Park differs from Tiger Stadium: Its wider green seats accommodate about 10,000 fewer fans and the double deck is gone. The outfield opens toward the downtown and fans walking by along Adams Street can see the action. A scoreboard dominates left field, and two levels of stands, separated by a double band of luxury boxes, run from foul territory in left to near first base, ending before a membership-only restaurant. Hardly any seats have obstructed views, though those in the upper deck are much farther from the action. Amenities abound—roomy restrooms, numerous concession stands, a Ferris wheel and carousel, lounges, and spacious walkways.

There is much I like about Comerica Park. It feels part of the downtown and after games the streets show life; people linger, intrigued by the exterior, by the decorative tiles and huge statues of tigers and baseball bats. I like the shape of the field. It is a pitcher's park, with deep alleys that approach 400 feet. And the club has honored its heritage with displays of memorabilia that tell of Cochrane and Crawford. But I don't like how the dugouts, which more than doubled in size, and the bullpens, behind the right-field fence, isolate fans from players, who no longer walk through the concourse to get to their cars. They have their own lot and their own entrance.

It's not Tiger Stadium but it has much to recommend it. Meanwhile the old ballpark's future remains uncertain. City officials say they want a developer to come forward with ideas; no one has yet. Earlier this month, Billy Crystal filmed *61\**, an HBO movie, there and fans again occupied the seats. I drive by occasionally. One time I saw Howard Stone flagging a few cars into his lot outside gate 9. There's a shuttle on game days that runs between Comerica and the old hangouts near Michigan and Trumbull. Incidentally, someone stole the signs that marked the intersection.

In Comerica, above left-center, stand larger-than-life sculptures of six Tigers: Cobb, Gehringer, Greenberg, and Kaline; Willie Horton, whose resemblance was added in July when the team retired his number 23; and Hal Newhouser, whom Dad faced all those years ago at Georgia Park.

"Yeah, that's how he looked," Dad said. "They got his motion right. He used to kick his leg out just like that."

Dad confirmed it with a nod.

He's been doing fine this year. He has a better hearing aid, which means I don't shout as much. Shortly after last season, he got a letter from his brother Herb, who is well in South Korea, retired from the Air Force and working as a civilian. He lives alone. "I get a Christmas card from Bucky every year and I hear from Bernice occasionally but never hear from Tom," Herb wrote. "How is Tom doing?"

I find some irony there, one missing uncle implying that the other has been out of touch. My mission succeeded at least on that front, bringing family together. Uncle Tom has become more a part of our lives. He and Dad went for lunch not long ago and this summer Tom and his wife traveled to California, where they visited Uncle Bucky, who is eighty-five and sharp of mind but unsteady of foot.

I gave my dad, my uncles, and my son Zack this manuscript before publication. I wanted them to read it. Recently, while we shot baskets in the driveway, I asked Zack what he thought.

"It's fine," he said.

"So nothing in there bothers you?"

"No."

He paused.

"But . . . you know where you wrote about me sitting a seat away at that game? Well, I really just wanted more room."

He smiled.

"My legs were smashed up against the seats in front of me."

His grin grew.

"It wasn't about all that other stuff."

"Oh really?" I said, raising my eyebrows.

"Yeah," he said. "I'm reading and all of sudden you're talking about something that happened on Mackinac Island about me riding a bike in front of you." He laughed and shifted into a lousy impersonation of my voice: " 'And I knew then my life would never be the same.' And I'm thinking, 'What? What's this? What are you talking about?' "

I started to laugh with him, which got him laughing harder, which got me laughing harder, and soon we couldn't shoot a basket.

"The seat was tight, Dad. That's all it was. Nothing else."

I've brought my sons to Comerica Park and they've enjoyed it. ("These seats have cup holders," one of them pointed out.) Though he couldn't name it, Zack said that something was missing, something intangible.

We usually sit along the third-base side with a clear view of the field. But my favorite spot takes me away from the action behind the upper deck near right field. There's a wide walkway where you can stand in the breeze and look down Columbia Street. And on the horizon you can see the top of Tiger Stadium, its darkened light towers silhouetted by the setting sun. And if you listen beyond the silence, if you listen with your heart, you can hear all sorts of things. You can hear your childhood, you can hear your dad and your uncles, you can hear Kaline connecting, you can hear the muted cheers of distant, ghost crowds, and you can hear your grandpa calling out from the bleachers. It's a beautiful sound, and it echoes across the decades.

## Acknowledgments

Many people helped bring this book to fruition. First, I am happily indebted to my agent, Philip Spitzer, for his faith and perseverance, and to my editor, Peter Wolverton, associate publisher of Thomas Dunne Books, for his skillful guidance and encouragement. Tim Wendel, Frank Provenzano, and Mike Varney provided invaluable assistance by reading and critiquing the manuscript, and Ernie Harwell extended numerous kindnesses. I also appreciate the efforts of Carolyn Dunkley and Joseph Rinaldi, both of Thomas Dunne. Further, I am thankful to Bob Costas, Elmore Leonard, Sparky Anderson, Larry Ritter, Dale Petroskey, Paul Dickson, and Tom Goldstein for their words, and to David Poremba of the Detroit Public Library, Carol Souchock of the Macomb County Library, Mark Cunningham, Tyler Barnes, Christina Branham, Melanie Waters, Steve Trudell, Steve Olsen, Sandy Stankiewicz, Bernice Cynowa, Dallas Felder, and my friends at the *Voice* newspaper for their courtesies and efforts behind the scenes.

At the stadium I enjoyed the company of hundreds of fans. In addition to those mentioned elsewhere in the book, I thank these sources: Jack Weigel, Tony Campeau, Jim and Jami Turano, Mike and Tim Gleason, Doris Bertalan, Bruce Kajo, Naoto Amaki, Robb Wilson, Andrew Alexander, Howard Krugel, Joel Scott, Brian Felder, Michael Foust, Michael Warholak, Michael Happy, Ron Studley, Jim Cleverley, Ric

Wellman, Jerry Keranen, Joe and Dorothy Stabile, Sharon Linsday, Yvonne Heacock, Ray Trella, Bruce and Jon Kaufman, Lamont Orr, Bill and Pete Leonard, Chuck Klonke, Bill Anderson, Lloyd Wallace, Allan Wood, Laura Kaminker, Jerry Curtsinger, Jack Golds, Chuck Morgan, Dave Pidgeon, Jack Cox, Shawn Ellis, Dwight Allen, Bill Robinson, Anthony Lewandowski, Geoffrey Rimshas, Dixie Tourangeau, Joe Kedra, and anyone else whose name escaped my notes. Finally, this book would not have been possible without the support of family, particularly my wife, Beth; our three sons, Zack, William, and Taylor; my father, Joe Stanton; and my uncles. I treasure them all.